CHANGING TRIBAL LIFE

About the Editor

An alumni of Patna University, Dr. (Mrs.) P. Sen has been teaching Philosophy at Mahila College, Chaibasa (Ranchi University) since 1971. She is presently the Reader and the head of the department at the same college. She has been awarded the Ph.D. degree on the Philosophy of K.C. Bhattacharyya. Her recent field of interest is tribal philosophy of life. She has published a monograph entitled Absolute, Self and Consciousness (1994) and has contributed several research papers to The Indian Philosophical Congress, Akhil Bharatiya Darshan Parishad, The Visva-Bharati Journal of Philosophy, Journal of Indian Council of Philosophical Research, Darshanik Traimasik etc.

CHANGING TRIBAL LIFE

A Socio-Philosophical Perspective

Edited by

PADMAJA SEN

CONCEPT PUBLISHING COMPANY PVT. LTD.
NEW DELHI-110059

ISBN: 978-81-8069-023-5

First Published 2003

Published and Printed by

Since 1974

Concept Publishing Company Pvt. Ltd.
A/15-16, Commercial Block, Mohan Garden,
New Delhi-110059 (India)
T : 91-11-41101460
E : publishing@conceptpub.com, *W*: www.conceptpub.com

Introduction

The papers in this monograph have been contributed to the National Conference sponsored by the UGC, Eastern Regional Office, Kolkata and organized at the Mahila College, Chaibasa on 21-22 March 2002. The theme of the Conference was 'Changing Tribal Life: A Socio-philosophical Perspective'.

Philosophizing tribal life may seem irksome to conventional philosophers. They might argue that such a particularistic approach is not generally the business of philosophy. But what emboldened the Department of Philosophy, Mahila College to conceive and organize the Conference was the accepted approach of studying the philosophy of particular spaces, demographies and cultures. Located in a predominantly tribal area and being exposed to their culture, advantaged the department in attempting this philosophizing of the tribal way of life. The idea was to create an epistemic corpus that may help us to understand their worldview.

The areas chosen for study in the Conference were: Concept of Tribe, Philosophy of Life, Concept of Value and Notion of Development. Since the study of tribal philosophy has not yet been attempted systematically I knew that resources of sister disciplines like history, anthropology, sociology and economics should help us in making a beginning. Hence this inter-disciplinary effort towards knowledge making.

The discussion begins with Dr. A. K. Sen's conceptualization of the Ho as a tribe. It studies the understanding of British ethnographers of the tribalism of Ho and also Ho imaging of the self. This knowledge of the self-image is necessary for formulating any philosophy. In her case study of the Oraons and Tana Bhagats, Dr. S. Das Gupta questions many of the common assumptions about tribe. She argues that many of the assumed specific tribal characteristics were in fact products of history being constructed by colonial officials, anthropologists and Christian missionaries.

The section on the tribal philosophy of life has in all eight papers. Sri M. Hembrom underlines that a happy living around natural surroundings, non-materialism and an open democratic worldview, which seeks to honour the dignity of a single individual, constitute the original tribal philosophy of life. But he rues the fall of the tribe from the essential strength of tribal culture mainly due to the baneful influence of an aggressive culture imported by outsiders.

Ms. R. Hebbar draws on her rich field experience of Ho village life to throw light on the significance of myth and ritual among the Ho tribe. She thus leads us into the Ho philosophy of the creation of man and this world.

Dr. P.P. Mahato highlights the reciprocity and assimilation in tribal worldview and challenges the very principle of listing people as scheduled tribe and the exclusion of other unscheduled but original peoples of Jharkhand even when the same philosophy of life governs both these sections of people.

Dr. A. Mahanta takes up the treatment system popular among the tribals in eastern India. He thus implies the notion of an alternative in the field of medicine, as Hembrom, Hebbar and Mahato seek to construct the cultural other that the tribe has to offer.

This otherness develops into Sri S. Sengupta's notion of distinct tribal identity, which he rightly emphasizes should form the basis of Indianness, honouring the identity of the marginalized among Indians.

When we broach the notion of identity we do not in Indian situation mean compartmentalization and insulation. The diachronic and synchronic readings lead us invariably into the reality of exchange and assimilation. Ms. T. Ghosh, Ms. B. Verardo and Dr. C.K. Paty have focused this.

Ms. Ghosh takes up the religion and art among the tribes of West Bengal. She stresses the essential primitive nature in the tribal artistic creations but does not fail to point out basic assimilative character at the folk level, both tribal and non-tribal, that goes into the making of a regional culture.

Ms. Verardo's fieldwork in Singhbhum virtually initiates us into a new world, the birth of a new religious cult and into an acculturation process that slowly but steadily enacts the drama of the detribalization of a tribe.

Dr. Paty studies the impact of Christianity in shaping and moulding the life of those who left tribal faith to adopt a new religion.

Dr. D. Guha and Dr. P. Sen address tribal concept of value. Dr. Guha weaves the philosophical idea of value as a backdrop to broach the basic value-ladenness in the 'professionals' as they approach such issues as the construction of Big Dams and projects. On the other hand, Dr. Sen seeks to focus how in tribal society the notion of value and the process of valuation is more existence-centric and has the preservation of its solidarity of a distinct demographic group as its main motive.

Ms. S. Topno and Sri S. K. Singh study the concept of development. Ms Topno highlights the dichotomy between the suggested conservationist approach of the tribe to natural resources and the destructive approach in the modern development policy. She questions the very purpose of the latter when it only brings denial and deprivation in tribal life. On the other hand, basically agreeing with Ms. Topno, Singh concentrates on what should be the appropriate philosophy of development that will ensure moral and material progress of tribal society.

I am conscious that the present work does not offer the readers a comprehensive reading of the socio-philosophical aspect of the changes occurring in tribal society. But the essays have been able at least to give us the very essences of tribal life that may inspire an elaborate philosophizing. The essences are reciprocity, assimilation, democratic living, a distinct philosophy of origin that integrates supernatural with natural world, a unique belief system that upholds harmony between man-nature, man-woman and adult-child, existentialist value system and a distinct notion of aesthetics, which philosophizes the amalgam of reality and imagination (Hembrom, Mahato, Sengupta, Hebbar, Sen, Ghosh and Topno in particular). The culture of upholding basic values of a happy community life and protecting the integrity of the community, as found among Santals (Sengupta), is in fact characteristic of tribal society in general. This worldview constitutes a distinct tribal identity, which have been highlighted through this book. There is also a clear assertion of the reality of this identity being submerged and muted by so-called civilized people, which caused '*Nirbakization*' (Hembrom and Mahato) as well as material distress and marginalization (Topno). One has to keep in mind this existentialist predicament of tribe at large.

Two essays in this volume (Das Gupta and Mahato) however caution us against the ethno centrism and politics that had structured tribal epistemology. This calls for further inter-disciplinary intervention. Sengupta rightly points out that archives are 'artificial artifects'and mere out side view is also not adequate. The need of the hour is an 'acquaintance with the inside views of tribal society'. I would only add that what is needed is perhaps an objective amalgam of both the 'inside' and 'outside'. The present work is just a humble beginning towards this.

PADMAJA SEN
Department of Philosophy
Mahila College, Chaibasa

Date : 22 March, 2002

Acknowledgements

As the Editor of this book I owe grateful thanks to many. It goes to the authors whose researches and presentation, even at a short notice, helped create a structure of knowledge, which was the need of the hour. The Conference and the publication would not have been possible without the financial support provided by the University Grants Commission, Eastern Regional Office, Kolkata. I am thankful to our Principal Dr. Veena Mahto for her encouragement and able leadership. To our former Principal Dr. S. Mahanty I am grateful because it was during her tenure that the Conference was planned and necessary sanction was procured. I gratefully acknowledge the sincere help of all teachers and office staff of our College, which made the Conference and Book a reality. I shall be failing in my duty if I do not particularly mention the names of Ms. S. N. M. Topno, Dr. U. Prasad, Dr. A. Mishra and Dr. K. C. Dey, who ungrudgingly shared the weal and woe that accompanied the entire course leading to this publication. I extend my heartfelt thanks to Sri D. N. Champia, Sri S. K. Sirka, Dr. P. P. Mahato, Sri C. B. Deogam, Dr. S. Sahay and Dr. Lokenath for their kind help. I am thankful to Fr. J. Cutinha of Tribal Research and Training Centre, Lupungutu for library facilities. I thank Sri Manish Garg of Hindustan Computer Arts, Chaibasa for his secretarial assistance. Last but not the least, I acknowledge the help of Dr. A. K. Sen for whatever he did for this book, but this labour of love can in no way be acknowledged with thanks.

Editor

Contents

Note on Contributors

Adikanda Mahanta is a Researcher from Chitrada, Mayurbhanj, Orissa.

Asoka Kumar Sen is Professor and Head, Department of History, Tata College, Chaibasa, Ranchi University, Ranchi.

Barbara Verardo is a Research Scholar, London School of Economics.

Chittaranjan Kumar Paty is Reader, Department of History, Tata College, Chaibasa, Ranchi University, Ranchi.

Debashis Guha is Reader, PG Department of Philosophy, Ranchi University, Ranchi.

Mondal Hembrom is Secretary, Ashin Dasgupta Institute of Tribal History, Kolkata.

Padmaja Sen is Reader and Head, Department of Philosophy, Mahila College, Chaibasa, Ranchi University, Ranchi.

Pashupati Prasad Mahato is an Assistant Anthropologist, Eastern Regional Centre, Anthropological Survey of India, Kolkata.

Ritambhara Hebbar is a Research Scholar, Department of Sociology, Delhi School of Economics, Delhi University Campus, Delhi.

Sangeeta Das Gupta is a Lecturer, Department of History, Visva Bharati, Santiniketan.

Sankar Sengupta is a Researcher, Ashin Dasgupta Institute of Tribal History, Kolkata.

Sunil Kumar Singh is a Research Scholar, Department of Sociology, Ranchi University, Ranchi.

S.N.M. Topno is Reader and Head, Department of Economics, Mahila College, Chaibasa, Ranchi University, Ranchi.

Tapashi Ghosh is a Lecturer, Jhargram Raj College, Jhargram, West Bengal.

1

Conceptualization of the Hos of Singhbhum as a Tribe

Asoka Kumar Sen

The attempt to conceptualize the Hos as a tribe may appear redundant at this point of time when the Constitution of India has long scheduled them as a tribe. But as a student of history we know that there has been a great debate why the tribals should be categorized as a tribe at all. There is the study of peasant-caste-tribe continuum, suggesting that a tribe could as well be identified as a peasant or caste group.[1] Then there is an attempt to understand the process and extent of Hinduization among them.[2] In a different context a tribe has also been identified as a colonial creation.[3]

This exercise at defining a tribe has largely been inspired by anthropology. Though anthropologists are not uniform in spelling the criteria this approach may seem a useful analytical tool in reading the past more meaningfully. Besides this reason, the present paper has also been inspired by an absence of any study on the concept of Ho as a tribe of the type of a case study on the Santals.[4] This paper seeks first to understand how British ethnographers had conceptualized the Hos of Singhbhum as a tribe. Next it selectively seeks to know the understanding of the Hos about themselves as an independent demographic category.

When we take up the British-day ethnography we notice three clear phases. The first was that of vague awareness about the Hos. Second was that of gradual unfolding of the people before administrator-ethnographers and preparation of cultural inventories by them, thereby recognizing their tribalism. Last was that of redefining and reconstruction of the tribe in the light of changes occurring in them under colonial rule and returning them to a British-filtered notion of tribalism.

Before elaborating the phases stated above I should clear my position. I beg to differ from the notion of tribe as a 'colonial creation'. It smacks of European ethnocentrism which does not as if accept the being ness of any people prior to colonial rule. This contention posits the colonial ethnography within the famous subject-object dichotomy. Just as the subjective idealists' contention that no material substratum exists in the mind of a subject, because to be is to be perceived, in the same fashion the British committed the 'fallacy of initial predication' when they thought that they constructed the tribe. As if it was non-existent before their intervention. The fallacy of initial predication consists in supposing the initial predicate or characteristics of an object known in the first acquaintance with it to be its defining characteristics. Similarly the British thought that the tribe (Ho in the present case) came into existence at the point of their initial contact with it. It is however equally conceivable that the tribe existed prior to and independent of colonial intervention.[5] In line with this argument I would like to say that tribalism was a pre-colonial notion, which the British were reconstructing instead of constructing it.

As I take up the first phase I find that in 1767, Vansittart, the resident of Midnapur, informed Verelest, the head of the Government in Calcutta, about 'a tribe of plundering banditti'. The vagueness in knowledge about the Ho continued as a result of which in 1819, Roughsedge, the British political agent, asked his assistant to collect all possible information about 'the extraordinary race called Larka'.[6] However, with the growth of knowledge the second phase began. Tickell and Dalton prepared their cultural inventories, which marked them out as a distinct people and defined their tribalism. But meanwhile the impact of British policies was bringing perceptible changes. Dalton made the glib observation, as I shall show below, of the capability of Hos in recreating themselves obviously under congenial British rule.

Meanwhile the need for conceptualizing a tribe had been gaining momentum since British Census operations and Ethnographic Conference of 1885 in Lahore. What were the avowed reasons? One was the urge to promote researches to be 'of some service to students of comparative ethnology in Europe'. The other was to apply the knowledge for the sake of 'good administration' and solving thereby 'possible social problems'.[7] There was however another stimulus. It was the discovery of the weakness in the policy of 'homogenization' particularly in the wake of anti-British uprisings of the 1850s. Dalton observed 'I think in this craving for homogeneity, the heterogeneous character of the component parts of the population of India should always be borne in mind'.[8] The need for preserving heterogeneity was felt all the more when the 'late census (1891) showed how rapidly the old aboriginal faiths are being effaced'.[9]

The underlying conservationist idea was noble. But at the same time one should not overlook the overriding imperialist consideration influencing British epistemic quest.[10] This was to highlight the areas of difference in the name of race, caste, religion and language to provide ideological counterpoise to Indian intelligentsia's search for unity in diversity. So the people had to be restored to this notion of recreated tribalism. With this introductory note I now seek to understand the colonial conceptualization of the Hos of Singhbhum as a tribe.

Ho as a Tribe

To do this I would like to apply some of the criteria used in anthropology to categorize a people as the tribe.[11] While examining how far British ethnographers were following these parameters in their identification of the Hos of Singhbhum we find that the application of the norms was more implicational than precise. This lack of precision was due first to changing tribal scenario over time. Next, being affected by imperialistic prerogatives the conceptualization served more the master than the muse. The result was that information provided was both cursory and often conflicting.

The Linguistic Identity

The ethnicity of the Hos was primarily woven around language. Tickell was perhaps the first to discover the linguistic basis of Honess identifying their dialect as separate from the Munda root.[12] This, with other cultural differences, which I shall show later, is suggestive of the transformation of a sub-ethnic group into an independent ethnic group. The emphasis on language/ dialect criterion encouraged Tickell and other ethnographers and linguists to undertake researches on the structure of Ho language. The result was Tickell's 'Grammatical Construction of the Ho Language' and 'The Vocabulary of the Ho Language' in 1840,[13] Dalton's tables showing different dialects of the Munda or Kol languages spoken in Chotanagpur and other places, 'Grammar of the Kol Language' in 1905 and 'Ho Grammar' in 1915 by Rev. A. Notrott and L.B. Burrows[14] respectively. Here the note of Burrows is significant. While citing the linguistic affinity among Hos, Mundas and Santals, he mentioned that change in time and environment brought linguistic differences among these groups which exalted 'Ho to the dignity of a distinct language'.[15]

The other aspect of this linguistic identity created the notion of two distinct linguistic poles–tribal and non-tribal. Dalton placed the Ho in the Kolarian linguistic group of which the main stock was Munda.[16] But remarkable fact is this that Kolarian language was projected not only as the linguistic other of the non-tribal ones but significantly as both political and cultural other also. Dalton observes 'Ethnologically their position is singular and interesting; speaking themselves the Kol language only, they occupy a basin whose barrier of hills restrains the flow and blending together of the three great Sanskrit derivatives Hindi, Bengali, and Uriya, which but for this obstacle of an isolated language would have found a trijunction boundary point in the centre of Singhbhum'.[17] If we read it in the context of power struggle between the Aryans and Kolarians over the Gangetic provinces[18] political overtone of the above polarization would become evident. The racial division of Indian population on the basis of language into Aryan and Munda-Dravidian families finally crystallized into an official linguistic policy by Grierson.[19]

British ethnographers and linguists had however to confront contrary evidences. Risley, who had faith in linguistic peculiarity as a marker, found 'a number of tribes concerning whose non-Aryan origin there can be no manner of doubt, have within recent times adopted Aryan dialects and abandoned their original language'.[20] About the Hos, Dalton found younger generation tending towards bi-lingualism compared to the susceptibility of seniors to their own dialect.[21] This was perhaps the result of the introduction of non-tribal languages like Hindi, Bengali and Uriya in the school curriculum since 1841 or contact with the people speaking these languages in Kolhan. Bilingualism became the pervasive trend of the subsequent decades.

This historical fact should not however detract us from the reality that the Hos of Singhbhum even in later years did not give up their mother tongue to adopt a non-Ho language. The compelling recent trend is their increasing solidarity around Ho language. This inspired Lako Bodra in the 1950s to formulate Ho script called Waran Kshiti and use this script to write books in Ho language. This effort reminds us of the birth of Olchiki script and spurt of an elaborate language movement ultimately claiming constitutional status for their language among Santals in and around Jharkhand. The Hos of Singhbhum have started a similar movement. These have made language a rallying point for them consolidating their linguistic identity as distinct not only from Munda or Santal but also other constitutionally recognized linguistic groups around.

Ho Geographical Space

Territoriality was the other determining norm. The argument was that demographic and spatial identities were co-terminus. Tickell informed that north Singhbum was the locus of the Hos immediately after they entered Singhbhum. But after a mutual agreement with the Porahat raj they later moved towards south Singhbhum and occupied major parts of it. Tickell argued that this was locally known as Hodesum, which the Hindus improperly called Kolehan.[22] But we notice a conflict in the naming of Ho territory. While in 1867 Dr. Hayes continued the use of the term desum, later Kolhan became the accepted name for the Ho territory.[23] Not only in nomenclature but in the area also we notice confusion. Kolhan, named Kolhan Government Estate since 1837, comprised 26 *pirs* (a group of villages) 'comprehending a tract of open undulating country, averaging from sixty miles in length north and south, from thirty five to sixty in breadth'.[24] But Dalton made a distinction between 'Ho or Larka Kol territory' and 'exclusively Ho territory'. The former was the entire district of Singhbhum lying to the south-east of Chotanagpur or between 20° and 23° of north latitude and 86° 53' and 85° 2' of east latitude comprising a total area of 4503 square miles, while out of the above area 1905 square miles constituted the latter.[25] This shows that they propounded the notion of a fluid and rigid Ho space.

What was the basis of delineating this administrative area? It was obviously the preponderant number of the Hos. Tickell's rough estimate was 60366 out of a total of 70653 i.e. about 85% of the total in 1840.[26] But about half a century later though the number rose to 175683 out of a total of 237320, the percentage share declined to 74.2%.[27] During Tuckey Settlement (1913-18) the official notion of Kolhan as the exclusive Ho land was further challenged when it was found that a large number of Kolhan villages had originally been founded and dominated by non-Hos.[28] Even then officially Kolhan continued to be accepted as the exclusively Ho land because of the demographic preponderance of the Hos and so non-Hos, more so non-tribals, came to be termed as *Dikus* or outsiders. This suggests that the British pinned their faith both on language and territory as decisive marks of Honess.

Even today the Hos feel emotive attachment towards Kolhan as their homeland around which their distinct culture had evolved over time and over which their very existence is at stake. This inspires them to claim Kolhan as an exclusive Ho land and retain the distinction between indigenes and outsiders.

Ho as a Pre-state Community

A tribe has been identified as a pre-state formation. We have some recent studies on the problem of state formation among other Jharkhand tribals.[29] Here we find the impact of

Sanskritization as a catalyst. But the application of the present test over the Hos is not possible for the lack of their definitive political history during pre-colonial period. From sparse evidence we can only deduce[30] that when Hos migrated into Singhbhum sometimes around the 10th century AD it was in the occupation of the Bhuiyans.[31] For the next few centuries they emerged as a strong political force, which helped them to defeat Bhuiyans and Saraks, to found Porahat raj and finally to register victories against the rajas of Porahat and Chotanagpur who wanted to subdue them between 1770 and 1800.[32] Meanwhile they had been able to evolve their polity of villages and pirs with Munda as the village and *Manki* as the *pir* head.

From this sparse ethnography colonial rulers could deduce that even if the Hos had ever been subjected under chiefdom, at the point of British contact their 'constitution of confederate village communities' or republics governed them.[33] So we can conclude that particularly after 1770 they had reached a stage when they enjoyed sufficient autonomy to venture the creation of a trans-*pir* body and integrate themselves under their indigenous state system. This political structure, adduced from British ethnography, however does not consciously conceptualize Hos as a pre-state formation. So we can say that this parameter does not form part, like language and territory, as the essential measure of Honess in the eyes of the British.

The contemporary situation however presents a paradox. Though Ho land is a part and parcel of Indian union the general trend among them is to consider their Manki-Munda system of village administration as the essential mark of their being a Ho and challenge any attempt at mainstreamization through the introduction of the Panchayati Raj.

Ho as a Distinct Cultural Group

This is an area where we find more conscious and precise reading of the Hos as a tribe by British ethnographers. This section will address such criteria as insulation, tribe vs. peasant, ethnic peculiarity and tribe as a pre-civilization community. I take up isolation criterion first. The isolation is mainly reasoned by the occupation of hilly and forested areas.[34] Another administrator introduced the notion of close affinity between nature and Ho rather nature's selection of the people as the inhabitant.[35] Tickell found that Larka Kol colonies 'are insulated, semi-barbarous and confined to the wildest parts of that country'.[36] Ho isolation even as late as the first decade of the twentieth century also figured in a later day official text.[37] I would like to point out that isolation as a demographic marker was stressed even when the British ethnographers could notice several and growing areas of mutuality.[38]

We are aware of the famous dichotomy between tribe and peasant current in anthropology. It argues that as their economy was also based on hunting, fishing, gathering and shifting cultivation tribal community should be regarded as pre-peasant.[39] Let us now seek supportive evidence from British-day accounts. Tickell noticed that at the time of breaking away from the parent Munda stock they were in a wild stage 'living chiefly by hunting'.[40] Till as late as the beginning of British rule they continued to live a 'nomad and predatory life', depending mostly on the natural products of the earth such as game, leaves and roots of trees and herbs which grew in the jungles.[41] However more abundant and compelling evidences support Hos as peasants. Immediately before the foundation of their rule the British found well developed villages abounding in cattle, sheep etc.[42] Tickell noted 'A Ho if he be worth three or four ploughs, lives in a very comfortable manner'.[43] If we move further ahead in time peasantization of the Hos seems more evident. D. M. Panna observes 'the Hos have become essentially agriculturists. They cannot be called good agriculturists, still they are agriculturists and must depend for their living on agricultural produce'.[44]

Peasantization was not however the only conscious material movement of the Ho society towards recreating themselves. They ventured into other vocations. We find Ho villagers trading their products in Kolhan markets, growing incidence of migration even to the tea gardens of Assam during British rule[45] and later Ho intelligentsia entering into literate professions or economic marginals moving beyond their homes for temporary and permanent jobs. Even then today a Ho feels emotive link both for his homestead and agricultural land be it very frail. So historically Ho and peasant may not be treated as two opposing poles nor does a Ho treat his peasantness as a disqualifier for his being a tribe.

The ethnic peculiarity of a tribe has been more systematically emphasized. They are treated as an altogether separate race mainly on the basis of contemporary physical anthropological findings.[46] Tickell, the first assistant political agent, called the Hos an 'aboriginal race'.[47] By the end of the nineteenth century Risley generically termed the tribals as belonging to a non-Aryan or Dravidian race or 'old aboriginal' similar to Dalton's enumeration of non-Aryan tribes.[48] The focus however shifted to tribals of Jharkhand being identified as 'an aboriginal savage race differing extremely in appearance, religion, language, and manners from the Hindu lowlanders of Hindustan'.[49] But at the same time the difference between a Ho and other tribals was also projected. Tickell found Ho and Munda differing 'not only in manners, dialect, and dress, but also in appearance. Dalton mentioned Hos of Singhbhum 'physically much finer people than the Bhumij, Santals or any other of the Kolarians'.[50] So in British eyes a Ho could be defined in terms of his physical difference both with a Hindu and other cognate tribes.

Added to this was the distinct social system, which argued the distinct cultural identity of the Hos of Singhbhum. Cultural inventories of Tickell, Dalton or Risley detail moral and material aspects of their culture to highlight their disjunction with Hindus, sometimes their superiority to Hindus also. These comments are revealing. About their non-Hinduness I have referred Dalton above. I shall now quote Tickell to prove their latter notion. He considered Ho women superior to Hindu women because 'They are well, and at times handsomely dressed, with a tasteful proportions of ornaments, without the stupid shyness and false modesty thought proper among Hindoo women'.[51] Next was the comparative context of village life. To quote 'while twilight lingers, their happy laughing voices, or the wild humming memory of their songs is heard; but no squabbling, no abuse or high words, no "Gallee," none of the vile traits of common Hindoostanee life, ever offend the ear'.[52]

The negative value judgment was however somewhat subjective. Even Tickell and other British ethnographers could notice subterranean current of Hinduization. Tickell informed about Hos adopting Hindu ceremonies, rites, festivals, and prejudices.[53] The current did not stop even later.[54] It appears therefore that a Ho could not be essentialized either as a Hindu or as a follower of any other non-tribal religion. In a recent paper we have argued that historically speaking tribals of Jharkhand evolved their religious ideas and practices, which showed borrowings from other religions also. But even then religion for a Ho, nay Jharkhand tribals, is not merely a matter of faith but has always been an assertion of distinct identity also.[55] If we enquire an educated Ho today his curt reply will be 'We are followers of *Sarna dhorom* and not a Hindu'. In recent years this exclusive religious identity has become a central item of their political assertion.

The last parameter will test whether a Ho belonged to a pre-civilization stage. In British ethnography expressions like primitive, savage and wild abound about tribals in general and Hos in particular.[56] In fact, the British in Kolhan set on the infamous dichotomy of wild and culture epitomizing in Roughsedge's infamous equation of the Larka village with tiger's den. In a recent unpublished paper we have argued that it was not simply a rhetoric but a rabid imperialistic conceptualization of a subject people that set off kind of a policy to capture them lock, stock and barrel.[57] This was so because the judgment maker did not consider contrary evidences available to him. Though we meet a later comment that there was not 'the remotest token of improvement in their way of living',[58] i.e. they continued to remain 'uncultured', the British had however to revise their attitude towards the community. To quote Dalton in support 'They appear to me to possess a susceptibility of improvement not found in the other tribes' and again 'there was every reason to suppose that the people were contented and making fair progress in civilization and prosperity'.[59] I do not want to make supportive evidences heavier. The above will make clear that once wild and uncivilized in British perception, the Hos in Kolhan progressively shunned their primitiveness and treaded the path of modernity. So the British could no longer conceptualize the Ho to be a tribe because of their uncivilized ness.

Conclusion

It thus becomes clear that the present-day anthropological criteria in defining tribal ness were consciously or unconsciously anticipated by British ethnographers in the conceptualization of the Hos. They defined the Hos essentially as a linguistic, pre-state and non-Aryan community having a well-defined territory of their own and a culture distinct in many respects from the neighbouring Hindus. They could not however hold on to their early identification of a Ho as a pre-peasant and pre-civilization people because even during pre-colonial situation Hos themselves had moved towards peasantness and modernity, the trends sharpening further during colonial rule. Even though there was a clear malleability in their conceptualization what we notice is that with the Census operations the British notion of Ho or any Indian tribe further crystallized to identify them as a demographic other of the Indian mainstream. But what we find here is that this quest was ideologically determined. Edward Said's observation on Orientalism is very evocative in understanding the politics behind the meaning of tribalism before colonial rulers. He says: "Additionally, the imaginative examination of things Oriental was based more or less exclusively upon a sovereign Western consciousness out of whose unchallenged centrality an Oriental world emerged, first according to general ideas about who or what was an Oriental, then according to a detailed logic governed not simply by empirical reality but by a battery of desires, repressions, investments, and projections'.[60] This reading relates that the conceptualization was not always factual but value-laden. So what I propose at the end is that any understanding of tribe should invariably be accompanied by the reading of the tribe in question about himself. Left to them tribals of Jharkhand, including Ho, would like not to call themselves a tribe but be known by the term Horo, Horoko or Ho. All mean man. This humanness marked them out from the animals sharing the forest. This is historically very suggestive. They mean that tribals were the original clearers and settlers of Indian forests. As such they are the adivasis or original or indigenes. Selective facts given above tell us that the tribals like the Hos of Singhbhum would more or less pin their distinct identity on language, territory and exclusive culture.

Notes and References

1. S. Sinha, 'Tribe-Caste and Tribe-Peasant Continua in Central India', *Man in India*, Vol. 45, No. I, (March 1965), pp. 57-78; A. Beteille, Tribe and Peasantry.
2. B.B. Chaudhuri, 'Society and Culture of the Tribal World in Colonial Eastern India: Reconsidering the notion of 'Hinduization' of Tribes' vide. H. Jha, *Perspectives on Indian Society and History. A Critique*, Manohar, Delhi, 2002, pp. 23-79.
3. T. Ranger, 'The Invention of Tradition in Colonial Africa', in E. Hobsbawm and T. Ranger, *The Invention of Tradition*, Cambridge University Press, 1996, pp. 211-262.
4. M.P. Yorke, 'Decisions and Analogy: Political Structure and Discourse among the Ho Tribals of India', Ph.D. Thesis submitted to the School of Oriental and African Studies, University of London, October 1976, pp. 60-64.
5. For the philosophical enumeration I am thankful to Dr. Mrs. Padmaja Sen.
6. L.S.S. O'Malley, *Bengal District Gazetteers Singhbhum,* Seraikela and Kharsawan, The Bengal Secretariat Book Depot, Calcutta, 1910, pp.31-2.
7. H. H. Risley, *The Tribes and Castes of Bengal*, Vol. I, Calcutta, 1981, p. iv.
8. E.T. Dalton, *Tribal History of Eastern* India (original title Descriptive Ethnology of Bengal), Cosmo Publication, Delhi, 1973, p. 3.
9. Risley, The Tribes, p. iii.
10. B.S. Cohn, *Colonialism and its forms of Knowledge*, Oxford University Press, Delhi, 1997, pp. ix, Chapter ii.
11. June H.H. Helm (ed.) *Essays on the Problem of Tribe,* University of Washington Press, 1968; A. Beteille, 'The Concept of Tribe with special reference to India' in A. Beteille, *Society and Politics in India-Essays in Comparative Perspective*, Oxford University Press, 1992, pp. 57-78.
12. Lt. S.R. Tickell, 'Memoir on the Ho desum' (improperly called Kolehan)', *Journal of Asiatic Society of Bengal*, Vol. XI, part II, 1840, p.803.
13. Lt. S.R. Tickell, 'Vocabulary of the Ho language,' *Journal of the Asiatic Society of Bengal*, Vol. IX, part II, July to December 1840, New Series, Calcutta, 1840.

14. Dalton, *Tribal History,* pp. 235-242.
15. L.B. Burrows, *Ho Grammar*, Calcutta, Catholic Orphan Press, 1915, Preface.
16. Dalton, *Tribal History*, p. 2.
17. *Ibid.*, p.179.
18. *Ibid.*, p.151.
19. G.A. Grierson, *Linguistic Survey of India*, Vol. IV, Motilal Banarsidass, Delhi, 1967, p. 1.
20. Risley, Tribes, p. xli.
21. Dalton, *Tribal History*, p.185.
22. Tickell, Memoir, p. 694. Tickell however did not reason the exact temporal origin, the mythic or real circumstance behind the name or its territoriality. Nor do we find any reason behind the semantic origin of Hodesum, even when desh, the root word is a non-Ho word.
23. A.K. Sen, Generalisations, Confusions and Reconstruction of Ho Historiography, Ashin Dasgupta Momorial Lecture delivered under the auspices of Ashin Dasgupta Institute of Tribal History, Calcutta, 1999, the section on The Concept of Ho land: Hodesum vrs Kolhan.
24. Tickell, Memoir, p. 699.
25. Dalton, *Tribal History*, p. 178.
26. Tickell, Memoir, p. 700.
27. J.A. Craven, *Final Report on the Settlement of the Kolhan Government Estate 1897,* Calcutta, 1898, p.18.
28. A. D. Tuckey, *Final Report on the Resettlement of the Kolhan Government Estate the District of Singhbhum 1913-1918,* Superintendent, Government Printing, Bihar and Orissa, Patna, 1920.
29. S. Sinha, 'State Formation and Rajput Myth in Tribal Central India', *Man in India*, Vol. 42, No. I, March, 1962; K. S. Singh, 'State Formation in Tribal Society: Some Preliminary Observations', *Journal of Indian Anthropological Society*, Vol. 6, 1971.
30. Tickell, Memoir, pp. 696-8.
31. *Ibid.*, pp. 696-7.
32. Dalton, *Tribal History*, p. 180.
33. *Ibid.*, p. 178.
34. Tickell, Memoir, pp. 694, 696.
35. F.B. Bradley-Birt, *Chota Nagpore A Little Province of the Empire*, London, 1903, pp. 85-6.
36. Tickell, Memoir, p. 694. See also Dalton, *Tribal History*, pp.184-5.
37. O'Malley, *The District Gazetteers*, pp. 31, 71.

38. Sen, Generalisations, section on the Notion of Insulation.
39. N.K. Bose, *Tribal Life in India*, New Delhi, 1971, pp. 4-5.
40. Tickell, Memoir, p. 695.
41. Tuckey, *Final Report*, p.118.
42. Sen, Generalisations, section on Ho or Kol as Larka.
43. Tickell, Memoir, p. 783. See also Dalton, *Tribal History*, pp. 189, 195.
44. Tuckey, *Final Report*, p. 119.
45. A. K. Sen, 'From Singhbhum to Assam : The Incidence of Labour Emigration, 1873-1918', in S. Roy (ed.), *History* (The University of Burdwan), Vol. II, No. I, 1999, pp.78- 88.
46. Risley, *Tribal History*, p. xxx.
47. Tickell, Memoir, p. 695.
48. Risley, *Tribes*, pp. I-iii; Dalton, *Tribal History*, p. 2.
49. Dalton, *Tribal History*, p. 164.
50. Tickell, Memoir, p. 803; Dalton, *Tribal History*, p. 190.
51. Tickell, Memoir, p. 784.
52. *Ibid.*, p. 788.
53. *Ibid.*, p. 803.
54. Tuckey, *Final Report*, p.128; M. Areeparampil, Socio-cultural and Religious Movements among the Ho tribals of the Singhbhum District of Bihar, in M. Miri (ed.), *Continuity and Change in Tribal Society*, Indian Institute of Advanced Study, Shimla, 1993, pp. 394-436.
55. P. Sen & A. K. Sen, 'Religion as Identity: Evolution of Religious Ideas among the Adivasis of Jharkhand', *Journal of Indian Council of Philosophical Research*, Special Issue on Philosophical Traditions in Regional Languages of India (forthcoming), pp. 243-254.
56. Dalton, *Tribal History*, p. 3; Tickell, Memoir, pp. 694-5.
57. A.K. Sen and P. Sen. 'Roughsedge's Equation and the Notion of Savage : Towards the Threshold of British Tribal Policy in Singhbhum (unpublished).
58. H.Ricketts (ed.), *Report on the district of Singhbhum. Selection from the Records of Bengal Government*, No. XVI, Calcutta, 1854, p.74.
59. Dalton, *Tribal History*, pp. 205, 183.
60. Edward Said, *Orientalism*, Penguin Books, 1985, pp. 5 and 8.

2

Constructing a Tribe
A Case Study of the Oraons and the Tana Bhagats in Late Nineteenth and Early Twentieth Centuries

Sangeeta Das Gupta

As the politics of backward groups, depressed classes and indigenous peoples assumes increasing importance in the Indian scenario, a study of tribes and tribalism, of tribal identity and tribal movements becomes relevant both for policy makers and for the academics. This paper deals with the concept of the tribe; it questions many of the assumptions that are commonly made by those who have studied, or continue to study tribes and tribal movements. In the imagining of the tribe in colonial and post-colonial India, there is a shared realm of suppositions: tribals are seen to be the oldest inhabitants of the land who have distinctive social institutions and land structures; as a people, they have been exploited, oppressed and subjugated by the non-tribals. This image, I argue, needs to be questioned. I narrate one episode of the history that produced the attributes of tribalism; I focus on the Oraon community, and the Tana Bhagat movement among the Oraons that began in 1914.

The first point that I would like to make is that perceived 'tribal' characteristics, a body of specific attributed characteristics were products of a history, a history in the making of which the colonial officials, anthropologists and Christian missionaries had participated since the early decades of the nineteenth century. A range of differences, across and within communities, thus receded to the background as administrators, anthropologists and missionaries created the tribe, the Oraons, and the Tana Bhagats. The specific structure of knowledge that was created as a result of their combined efforts was the product of an intermeshing of several institutional and intellectual influences – biblical and evangelical concerns, the doctrines of evolutionism, diffusionism, functionalism, romanticism and positivism, and the demands of governance and thence intervention. Intellectual moorings, ideological positions and the colonial experience of governance converged and conflicted to constitute the quintessential image of tribe.[1]

Secondly, theorizations by historians studying tribal protest have remained constricted within the shared realm of suppositions inherited from colonial times. Writings on tribal movements, and the Tana Bhagat movement, are structured by, and may be located within this paradigm. Rarely have debates on tribalism and ethnicity, so popular in African studies, been discussed in the Indian context, the exceptions being Susan B.C. Devalle's *Discourses of Ethnicity: Culture and Protest in Jharkhand*[2] where she sees the tribe as essentially a construct, a colonial category. Usually however, tribal protest in Indian *historiography*, and in this case tribal conflict in Chotanagpur, is inevitably viewed as a united resistance of essentially homogenous tribal groups or adivasis against the infiltration of 'non-tribals' into their territory. The assumption implicit is that the economic interests of these groups were inherently antagonistic. Often uncritically accepting the substance and language of colonial administrative records, missionary and anthropological writings, historians have perceived tribal communities as almost homogeneous units, united in an opposition to alien and unacceptable elements that had entered their lands. K.S. Singh therefore identifies in the Tanas a 'peasant consciousness'[3]; B.B. Chaudhuri finds an economic basis to the 'rebel tribal consciousness'[4]; Prabhu Prasad Mohapatra, drawing upon the juridico-economic language of the colonial state, sees in the 'agrarian regimes in Chotanagpur...a continuous conflict between landlords and tenants', a 'class struggle'[5].

For those who idealize community histories, and look beyond the confines of socio-economic contexts and economic determinism in their attempts to understand tribal movements, there exists a necessary contradiction between 'capital' and 'community'[6]. Community movements, and in this case tribal movements, reflected the natural solidarity of the community 'They claim precisely the right against externality and secession, they seek determinate existence precisely in "property" and "representation" through collectively recognized heads, they speak in the language of love and of self-recognition through the free surrender of individual will to others in the community'.[7] In the name of theory then, as Sumit Sarkar points out, there has appeared in the present approach of the subalterns, a tendency 'towards essentialising the categories of 'subaltern' and 'autonomy', in the sense of assigning to them more or less absolute, fixed, decontextualised meanings and qualities'.[8]

My study of the tribe and the Tana Bhagat movement questions this homogeneity and autonomy/independence that has been attributed to the tribe in both these sets of studies. It recognizes the importance of tracing Oraon and Tana opposition to zamindars, banias and the British state, but it suggests that conflict must also be located within the internal hierarchy of the community. In the Oraon community, the *bhuinhars*, were the holders of privileged tenures; in addition, as members of the *panch* and as claimants to the traditional offices of the *pahan* (Oraon priest), *pujar* (one who helped the *pahan* in his duties) and *mahto* (village representative in secular affairs), they were the sources of authority within Oraon society. British intervention in Chotanagpur, their administrative arrangements and agrarian legislations, only intensified the already prevalent hierarchies in the Oraon community. As they attempted to preserve custom, and at the same time fit it into an agro-economic determinism, they identified in the agrarian population the leaders of the community - the *bhuinhars*. They thus directly promoted the interests of only a particular section of the Oraon tribe. It was the special position of these *bhuinhars* that the Tanas also challenged through their movement. The two seemingly disparate realms of Tana protest – an opposition to the *pahan*, *mahto*, and to the world of spirits and ritual celebrations, and a resistance to the landlords, *banias* (money-lenders) and the Raj – were thus interlinked. The Tanas articulated the ideology of a marginal group within Oraon society to redefine its identity, its past, its future. Their identity was as much a part of a larger discursive process of classification and codification by the colonial state and its allies. An analysis of this process is essential for an understanding of tribal protest.[9]

I

The Story and Tana Precepts

The Tana Bhagat movement began in April 1914. Jatra, a twenty five year old youth, proclaimed that he had received a divine message from *Dharmes*, the Supreme God of the Oraons.[10] Jatra was to be the king and his followers were to share the kingdom; the Tana sect was to be markedly different from the Oraon community. Oraon religion was to be purged of evils like ghost-finding and exorcism, belief in *bhuts* or spirits, animal sacrifice and liquor drinking.[11] Jatra's followers were to work no more as coolies or labourers for men of other castes or for the government.[12] They were also to stop the payment of rent to landlords. God would provide for them, and a single grain of rice would satisfy a person's hunger.[13] Because of the impending destruction of the world when earthly possessions would be the only hindrances, disciples of the faith were asked to purify themselves by discarding household equipments, agricultural implements and ornaments into the river, as purificatory sacrifices to the goddess Ganga.[14]

As the new faith began to spread to Ghagra, Gumla and Bishnupur, *mantras*, that had originally referred only to ghosts, soon came to include Babhans (a high caste in Bihar), Mussalmans and the English in their list of evils.[15] In end-1915, the movement had spread to Mandar and Kuru; due to intermittent acts of violence, a panic was created there among local zamindars and 'non-aboriginals'. Particularly harassed were the zamindars, their servants being beaten and turned out of jungles when they attempted to collect wood. As appeals to the 'German Baba' were particularly marked in this phase, a battle between the Germans and the English was predicted; in this, the Germans would win and they would then march to India. In the meantime, the British may turn against the *bhagats* (devotees), but their bullets would be turned into water.[16]

In 1919, Tana activity resumed under a new leader, Sibu Oraon. Sibu had been instructed by *Bhagawan* to leave his home and family and wander all over the world in order to reform it. The Raj was shortly to be restored to the Oraons. *Bhagawan*, Sibu claimed, would send him letters. Pieces of foolscap in illegible Hindi writing, distributed to the police, expressed some of Sibu's ideas: 'The Mussalman kill cows, so their bones will be broken… Marwaris sell cloth at a very high price, so their homes should be burnt… Zamindars realize taxes and keep dancing girls, they should be turned out…'.[17]

A movement that had spread over Ranchi, Palamau, Hazaribagh, and parts of north Bengal, and had spanned a considerable period of time, and in which there were moments of momentum and ebb, there were leaders who differed in their doctrines. Yet, certain essential principles marked the Tana faith: ghosts and spirits were to be purged; the traditional leadership of the *pahans* and *mahtos* was to be questioned; sacrifices, violence and non-vegetarianism were to be abhorred. In addition, the Tanas questioned their subordination to the zamindars, *illaquadars* (those who had been granted land by the Maharajah of Chotanagpur in exchange of services that were to be rendered) and banias, and to the Christians and the British state. Their demands related, among other things, to issues of land, rent and a variety of other forms of dues.

The story of Tana protest thus reflects a complex of seemingly contradictory pressures that coexisted within the movement. Their movement drew upon a collective Oraon identity and, at the same time, distanced itself from some of the Oraon traditions and practices. Tanas questioned the supremacy of the *pahan*, *pujar* and *mahato*, denounced the prevalent Oraon practices of spirit worship, witchcraft, sacrifice, non-vegetarianism and festivity, and presented a critique of settled agriculture. Simultaneously, they identified the enemy outside the Oraon community: they critiqued the privileges of the zamindars and banias, and the exactions imposed by them. These seemingly divergent practices, I seek to argue, were interlinked; these were expressions of an integrated Tana protest against relations and hierarchy that were based on claims to lineage and ownership of land.

II

A Brief History of Chotanagpur and its Agrarian Terrain

To understand the Tana Bhagat movement, one needs to enquire into the gradual entrenchment of the British in the region, the structure of landed power in Chotanagpur, and the location of the Oraons within its agrarian terrain. But, more importantly, one needs to study the processes through which the already prevalent hierarchies in Oraon society were strengthened and recast as a result of colonial intervention. Colonial records, particularly settlement reports, reflected the rural scenario but, I argue, reconstituted it as well. The intervention of the Raj altered and reconstituted tenurial relations, administrative arrangements and juridico-legal structures dismantled rural hierarchies and traditional methods of control and management. The Tana Bhagat movement, with its varying dimensions, needs to be located within this context.

In the early days of British contact with Chotanagpur, the Raja of Chotanagpur or the Raja of Khukhra, as he was then referred to, was allowed to administer the country on the payment of a certain amount of revenue to the British. Chotanagpur, it needs to be pointed out, then a part of the province of Bihar, was included within the British dominion after 1765.[18] Relations between the Raja and the British were prone to strains from the very outset. By 1806, Captain Roughsedge, the Commandant of the Ramgarh Battalion, had painted in his letter of 27 October 1806, a 'lurid picture of the disorders prevalent in the district, the recalcitrance of the Raja, and the general inefficiency of British control'[19]. British intervention, henceforth, was steady and penetrating. In 1809, police *thanas* (stations) were established which were placed under the control of the Magistrate of Ramgarh; in 1823, excise duties, the most important source of revenue in the district, was resumed by the British; in 1833, a number of administrative reforms were introduced in the region: a regular system of police and courts was established, and an Agent to the Governor-General was appointed in the region in whom was vested the control over the administration of justice and the collection of revenue. In 1854, a new official who was to be appointed by the local government replaced the Agent; he later assumed the title of Commissioner.

British intervention thereafter took the form of legislative enactments as conflicts between the zamindars on the one hand, and the ryots on the other, necessitated the determination of a procedure for the disposal of revenue suits, and for the realization of revenue. The Bhuinhari Act of 1869 was followed by surveys between 1869-1880; the survey and settlement operations in Ranchi extended from 1902 to 1910, and the Chotanagpur Tenancy Act was finalized in 1908.[20] And yet, administrative efforts at recording the customary rights of landlords and villagers had paradoxically led to the enhancements of rents and *rakumats* (various payments in kind and miscellaneous cesses), along with a conflict that arose over the rights to the jungles. Further, lines of communication between an outlying province and the metropolis had introduced newer socio-economic forces in the region and forged a closer link between land, capital and market. Traders and moneylenders or the *mahajans*, *sahus* and *banias*, zamindars, intermediate tenure-holders and ryots, lawyers and petty traders, now entered the credit, tenurial and tenancy markets.[21]

Contentious relations between the landlord and the ryots thus had a long history. In the perception of the Oraons and Mundas, who constituted the agricultural population of the region, they were the proprietors of the soil who had lost their land to the outsiders. From the outset, the Tana Bhagat movement was marked by a protest against landed elements. This protest took the form of refusals to pay rent and offer *begari* (praedial services), assaults on the zamindar, a forcible cultivation of his lands and the cutting of crops, and appeals to the state through the submission of pamphlets, petitions and memorials. The Tanas then, on the one hand, had articulated feelings of outrage that were shared by other members of the agricultural community against the infiltration of outsiders into their land; it was this protest that reinforced community solidarity.

III

Tanas against *Bhuinhars*

Yet, Tana interest in land went beyond an anti-zamindari campaign. Their antagonism towards the zamindars and banias, and towards the existing power structure, fused with indignation against an agrarian system and the hierarchies that it sustained. Perceiving their oppression and subjugation to be a consequence of plough agriculture, they critiqued the pattern of settled agriculture that veered around the plough, agricultural festivities, elaborate customs and dancing, and proposed a return to their past of shifting agriculture and forest dwelling. In their myths and legends they linked their subjugation and impoverishment to a history of their transformation from shifting cultivators to plough agriculturists.[22] This had initiated a process of decline, a movement from a state of well-being to a state of impoverishment. It had provided the context in which their degradation and subordination was complete and their freedom was lost. Their escape lay therefore in a renunciation of the basis of their subjection. It was thus an attachment to pre-agricultural forms that Jatra's affirmations indicated: he had asked his followers to give up the ploughing of fields since it entailed cruelty to cows and oxen, but did not save the Oraons from famine and poverty. God would provide for them, he stated. 'A single grain of rice would be enough to satisfy a person's hunger… a handful of rice grains if scattered on this land would produce enough to fill a grain attic. Household equipments, agricultural implements and ornaments were to be discarded by his disciples as part of the purificatory acts that would welcome the millennium.[23] Tanas, it needs to be noted, came from the categories of the insignificant in Oraon society: the non-occupancy ryots and the under-ryots.[24] Their grievances, when explicitly expressed, centred on the issues of rent and *begari* (a number of day's labour, arbitrarily fixed, performed by the ryot for his landlord). Land if cultivated would be on the *bataia* (a system of rent payment where a part of the produce was paid as rent), they asserted.

Who then were those that represented the sources of authority within Oraon society and whose privileges the Tanas had, but never publicly, critiqued? The Tana opposition to the hierarchies within Oraon society, I argue, needs to be constructed from a careful analysis of their tenets, practices and ideology. The Tanas questioned the supremacy of the *pahan*, *pujar* and the *mahto*; they rejected the spirit world, sacrifices and festivity; their search was for a past that predated a settled agricultural economy. These facets, different and yet interlinked, were expressions of an integrated Tana protest against social relations and hierarchy that were based on claims to lineage and ownership of land.

This section seeks to analyse a process of internal differentiation that was strengthened in Oraon society with the intervention of the British in Chotanagpur. The support extended to the *bhuinhari* community by the British, and the codification and implementation of the Bhuinhari Act of 1869 had deepened not only the conflict between the *bhuinhars* and the *illaquadars*, but had also accentuated the differences between the *bhuinhars* and non-*bhuinhars* in Oraon society. The Tanas, as non-*bhuinhars*, now opposed the Bhuinhari Settlement and those who were recognized as exercising these *bhuinhari* rights.

Who, then, were these *bhuinhars*? What was the nature of conflict that arose within the Oraons as a community?[25]

In the agrarian terrain of Chotanagpur, the *bhuinhars*, or those who held *bhuinhari* lands, were a community that the British regarded as significant. In addition to the *manjhihas* ('tenures' of the zamindars) and the *rajhas* ('tenancies' of the ryots), the officials had identified in Chotanagpur a third 'class' of rights on land, the *bhuinhari*. *Bhuinhari* rights, they argued, were exercised by descendants of the original clearers of the soil. This land was held rent-free with only services attached to it, or at a quit-rent. In this category were also included the *bhutkheta*, *dalikatari*, *pahnai* and *mahtoi* tenures. *Bhutkheta*, dedicated to the worship of spirits, was held by a *bhuinhari khunt* (clan) for the propitiation of the family spirit, or by the *pahan*, on behalf of the village community, for the propitiation of village spirits. The *dalikatari* and *pahnai* lands were also held by the *pahan* for the same purpose. *Mahtoi* lands were service tenures held by the *mahto* or the village headman.[26]

For the British, who from their own experience in their homeland were accustomed to classifying the rural population into 'landlords' and 'tenants', understanding the prevalent land system in Chotanagpur was problematic since there existed in this region older customary and community rights over land. Yet, for the administrators, even what was customary was to be fitted into their understanding of tenurial and tenancy classifications. Hence, along with the privileged lands of the landlords, *bhuinhari* was, on occasions, classified as 'tenures'[27]; elsewhere it appeared, along with *raiyati* lands, as 'cultivating tenancies'.[28] While seeking to resolve this discrepancy, Reid wrote: 'They [the *bhuinhari*] are tenures under the law; but, for practical purposes, they may be regarded as *raiyati* tenancies...'[29]

Bhuinhari rights entered the perceived realm of custom that the British had intended to recognize, contend with and preserve; those who exercised these rights were therefore to be protected. At a time when colonial administrators in Chotanagpur were trying to determine and uphold rental obligations and occupancy rights based on custom, here was a community which symbolized the prevalence of customary law in Chotanagpur. In keeping with the special position accorded to the *bhuinhars*, it was their voice that the administrators chose to hear. *Bhuinhars* were viewed as the representatives of the Kols; a redressal of their grievances was seen as a step towards establishing amicable relations between zamindars and ryots. Missionaries who were actively involved with tribal communities gave a sanction and support to official argument. Anthropological theories attributed to this shared structure of thought a coherence and credibility. The Oraon claims to land were perceived in the following manner: the pioneer families – nuclear or extended – who had cleared the jungles were the *bhuinhars* who held rent-free land; the descendants of these original reclaimers of the soil held privileged tenures and had a social precedence over later Oraon settlers; the subsequent Oraon settlers being called *jeth* ryots or ordinary ryots, depending on whether they were earlier or later settlers.[30] History perceived thus, authenticated a hierarchized structure in tribal society.

In this context, the missionary support to the *bhuinhars* merits attention. Upholding primarily the interests of the *bhuinhars* or the original cultivators over those cultivators who held only *rajhas* lands, the missionaries argued that the Kols, especially the *bhuinhars*, and not only the native Christians, were oppressed and wronged in different by the *jagirdars* and *thikadars* (contractors). Most of the cases cited in missionary pamphlets and memoranda, and discussed in their meetings and conferences inevitably centred around *bhuinhari* and their grievances.[31]

Constructed myths and the reality of British intervention thus vested on the *bhuinhars* a unique position in Oraon society. At a time when land was becoming increasingly valuable in Chotanagpur, particularly in view of a decreasing arable space and the consequent struggle over forest lands, the *bhuinhars* attempted to control land in order to counteract their economic insecurities. British policy helped in their endeavours. As informants of local custom, they could reaffirm their dominance in Oraon society and, at the same time, contest the rights of the zamindars to land. What could be the results of such a development for the other sections of the Oraon community? A privileged group had emerged from within the *bhuinhars* that took advantage of a tradition accorded privileged status and the settlement operations to stake a claim as an upwardly mobile group in Chotanagpur, and thus the conflict between the *bhuinhars* and non-*bhuinhars*, the privileged and unprivileged, within Oraon society was further aggravated. Once *bhuinhari* cases ended, the struggle for *rajhas* began. Once again, in the assertion of their rights, *bhuinhars*, as a privileged community from among the Oraons, were in a position to deprive the under-ryots of their lands. The groups of non-occupancy and under-ryots to which the Tanas belonged were in a particularly vulnerable position because they now came under the social and economic control of select *bhuinhars*, and faced in addition the threat of ejection. *Bhuinhars*, who participated directly in the cultivation of their lands, often chose to replace this section by members of their own families. Conflicts between the privileged and the marginalized sections of the Oraon community therefore became particularly marked after the intervention of the colonial state and its allies, the missionaries, in Chotanagpur. The Tana Bhagat movement expressed therefore, not only a protest of the Oraons against the non-Oraons, it was as much a response to the tensions and hierarchizations which arose within Oraon society. Their protest was, however, not always overtly expressed, as I have already pointed out. At one level, the Tanas identified themselves with the rest of the Oraon community in a commonly expressed outrage against the 'outsiders'.

IV

Against a World of Spirits, Sacrifice and Festivity

The difference between the *bhuinhars* and the non-*bhuinhars* was reflected not only in wealth and control over resources, but also in social status and authority. In the Tana rejection of the supremacy of the *pahan*, *pujar* and the *mahto,* and of the world of spirits, sacrifices and festivity is indicated, I argue, a search for a past that predated a settled agricultural economy and the hierarchies that it sustained.

The spirit world was a primary focus of the Tana attack. While Oraons saw the spirits as a part of a system that sustained the rules and norms of the community and protected it from evil, the Tanas blamed the spirits who had been regularly propitiated for having failed to alleviate the socio-economic conditions of the Oraons. By denying the dual nature of beneficence and malevolence that the Oraons had attributed to these spirits and denouncing these as wholly evil, and by breaking the relationship of reciprocity between the living and the dead, the Tanas marked a sharp break from prevalent Oraon customs. *Dharmes* had emerged as the sole protector; only he could ensure prosperity and abundance.

At the same time, sacrifices, usually elaborate affairs which were an integral part of Oraon worship, were forbidden by the Tanas, along with those who played the central role in the arena of festivals and *jatras* (ritual celebrations): the *pahan* or *baiga*, the *bhandari* or *pujar*, and the *mahto*. Interestingly, these offices were the exclusive preserve of the *bhuinhari khunts* (clans), and even the majority of spirits were regarded as having belonged to the *bhuinhari khunts*, or could be appeased only in the presence of the *pahan*.[32] Inherent in the Tana opposition to Oraon popular practices and the spirit world is thus a rejection of the traditional sources of authority in the Oraon community. The implicit Tana antagonism towards *bhuinhars* assumes an added significance when we consider that their movement around the time of settlement operations during which the *bhuinhars* were accorded a privileged status over the later Oraon settlers; and the *pahan*, *pujar* and *mahto*, regarded as the natural leaders of the people had emerged as the informants of custom and tradition. Tradition had accorded to the *mahto* and the *pahan* the joint right to settle vacant raiyati lands, and this further aggravated the conflicting interests of the *bhuinhars* and the non-*bhuinhars*. The Tana irreverence towards rights and ceremonies that aimed at ensuring safety at important moments of an individual's life, and at each stage of the economic pursuits of the community, indicated, therefore, a resistance to the Oraon agrarian and settled economy.

A similar attitude was expressed in the Tana refusal to accept the jurisdiction of the *panch* (administrative body among the Oraons) that was constituted by *bhuinhars*. Tana disputes and differences were required to be settled by the *mandali* (congregation), and later by the *panchayat* (assembly). Tanas not abiding by their decisions were excommunicated. Significantly, the *pahan* and the *mahto* were as much against the movement that had sought to challenge and dismantle their authority. It was reported that 'the mahtos and pahans of the village affected did not join, and disapproved of the attitude of the younger men; they were afterwards found useful in checking the whole movement'.[33]

Conclusion

Tanas, I have argued in this paper, articulated the ideology of a marginal group within Oraon society. Their movement expressed the response of a section within the Oraon community to outsiders – the zamindars, the banias, the missionaries and British administrators–who had entered the Oraon land, to Oraon traditions, belief structure, rituals and practices, and to colonial penetration in Chotanagpur. This paper thus seeks to inquire into the link between two processes: a process in which administrators, anthropologists and missionaries defined and determined who an Oraon was and what were his rights; and a process through which a historically constituted community of Tanas responded to the influence of different worlds. While the former was not hegemonic, Tana response, in turn, was not autonomous.

Notes and References

1. For a detailed discussion of this point, refer to my Ph.D. dissertation. Sangeeta Das Gupta, 'Reordering of Tribal Worlds: Tana Bhagats, Missionaries and the Raj', Ph.D. Dissertation, *Centre for Historical Studies*, Jawaharlal Nehru University, 1998.
2. Susana B.C. Devalle, *Discourses of Ethnicity : Culture and Protest in Jharkhand,* Sage Publications, New Delhi, 1992.
3. K.S. Singh, 'Tribal Peasantry, Millenarianism, Anarchism and Nationalism: *A Case Study of the Tana Bhagats in Chotanagpur,* 1914-25', Social Scientist, Vol. 16, 1988, p. 36.
4. Benoy Bhusan Chaudhuri, 'The Story of a Tribal Revolt in the Bengal Presidency: The Religion and Politics of the Oraons, 1900-1926', in Adhir Chakrabarti, ed., *Aspects of Socio-economic Changes and Political Awakening in Bengal*, Calcutta, 1989, p. 55.
5. Prabhu Prasad Mohapatra, 'Class Conflict and Agrarian Regimes in Chotanagpur, 1860-1950', *The Indian Economic and Social History Review (IESHR),* Vol. 28:1,1991, p. 35.
6. Partha Chatterjee, *'Communities and the Nation'* in his The Nation and its Fragments, New Delhi, 1993, pp. 220-239.
7. *Ibid.*, pp. 231-32.
8. Sumit Sarkar, *'The Decline of the Subalterns'* in Writing Social History, New Delhi, 1997, p. 88.
9. For a detailed study of the Tana Bhagat movement in its various facets, refer to Sangeeta Das Gupta, 'Reordering a World: The Tana Bhagat Movement, 1914-1919', *Studies in History*, 15, 1, n.s. 1999.
10. A. John, 'Eine Reise nach Chechari' [A Journey to Chechari], Die Biene auf dem Missionsfelde fur Missions-freunde und Missions Vereine (hereafter Die Biene auf dem Missionsfelde), No. 1, January, 1928, p. 65. This journal translated as 'The Bee from the

Missionfields: *For Missionary Friends and Missionary Associations'*, published from Berlin, was the annual missionary journal of the German Evangelical Lutheran Mission (later renamed Gossner Evangelical Lutheran Mission).

11. Sarat Chandra Roy, *Oraon Religion and Customs*, Calcutta, 1928, p. 341. Roy's account of the movement draws upon a government report. This report titled 'Oraon unrest', which unfortunately does not have a reference number, is found among Roy's private papers [hereafter RPP], located at the office of the *Man in India* [hereafter MII], Ranchi.
12. Bihar and Orissa Government, Political Department, Special Section, File No. 54 of 1925.
13. A. John, 'Eine Reise nach Chechari', p. 64.
14. W. Dehmlow, 'Ein falscher Prophet in Bahar-Barwe [A False Prophet in Bahar-Barwe], Die Biene auf dem Missionsfelde, No. 11, November, 1914, p. 151.
15. 'Oraon unrest', RPP, MII, Ranchi.
16. Bihar and Orissa Government, Political Department, Special Section, File No. 1165 of 1916.
17. Bihar and Orissa Government, Political Department, Special Section, File No. 86 of 1919.
18. The Nawab of Bengal granted the dewani of Bengal, Bihar and Orissa to the British in 1765.
19. John Reid, *Final Report on the Survey and Settlement Operations in the District of Ranchi 1902-10,* Calcutta, 1912.
20. For a brief history of the expansion of British power in Chotanagpur, refer to Reid, *Final Report,* pp.13-50.
21. The conflict between the Oraons and the non-Oraons has been discussed in detail in my 'Reordering a World: *The Tana Bhagat Movement*, 1914-1919, pp. 9-17.
22. For a discussion of Oraon and Tana myths, refer to my 'Reordering of Tribal Worlds', pp.181-87.
23. Dehmlow, '*Ein falscher Prophet in Bahar-Barwe'*, pp. 151-52.
24. F.A.B. Taylor, *Final Report on Revisional Survey and Settlement in Ranchi 1927-35,* Patna, 1938, p. 42. Four categories of ryots were identified by Taylor: occupancy ryots, ryots having *khuntkatti* (a local variant of *bhuinhari* usually held by the Munda tribe), non-occupancy ryots and under- ryots.
25. For a more detailed elaboration of the argument, refer to my '*Reordering a World: The Tana Bhagat Movement*, 1914-1919, pp. 17-24.
26. Reid, *Final Report*, p.121.

27. *Ibid.*
28. *Ibid.*, p.118.
29. *Ibid.*, p.96.
30. S.C. Roy, *The Oraons of Chota Nagpur : Their History, Economic Life and Social Organization,* (Ranchi : 1915); reprint (Calcutta, 1972), pp. 66-68.
31. An Inquiry into the Causes of the Land Question in Chutia Nagpore and an Attempt to Devise Means for its Solution by the 'Vorstand' of the German Evangelical (Gossner's) Mission in Chutia Nagpur. Most Respectfully Submitted to Her Majesty's Government, Benaras, 1889, p.10.
32. Roy, *Oraon Religion and Customs*, pp. 68-71.
33. 'Oraon Unrest', RPP, MII, Ranchi.

3

A Socio-Philosophical Change in Tribal Life

Mondal Hembrom

Before taking up the question of socio-philosophical change in tribal life, I would like to highlight the historical perspective of the mode of tribal life and livelihood in a nut shell. What we find is that while tribals have been maintaining their languages, cultures and traditions, since long every effort has been made to arrest the flow of their culture and traditions by others. Though in many cases it has somewhat succeeded in distorting their way of life, it could not stop the flow of the stream. Still these are echoed through their songs, *bintis* in the hills and hillocks, river and rivulets and in the veins of their mother-forests. Sweet beating sound of *dhamsa-madol* still reverbates the forest land. Still now the drunken Nature sings in a melodious tune in Sarhul, Karam, Saharay, Bandana etc. festivals. In the moonlit night when shadow plays with light, even the gods and goddesses from heaven, as if, participate in dance and merry-making with the mortals on the earth. This *adivasi* culture is different from Hindu culture if viewed from tribal mythological point of view. The notion of creation of earth in both these cultures is different. *Adivasis* believe that *Sari* or the truth was not established in a day or two, it took years together. *Sari* is the religion of the *adivasis*.

Tribals have a rich tradition of migration into Jharkhand. In ancient times Jharkhand was quilted in forest when the beasts reigned over the forest land. Wandering from *Hihiri Pipiri* or being driven out by the aliens, the Kherwals (ancient name of the austric group of people) were compelled to enter into the dense forests. They developed their own culture without being affected by others. Hunter wrote 'The Santal owes nothing of his skill in husbandry to the Aryans. He has crops of his own, implements of his own, own system of cultivation and an abundant vocabulary of rural life not one word of which he has borrowed from his superior race who ousted him from his heritage in the valley'. This life was essentially village-centric. The tribal of middle-east India cleared the forests, reclaimed lands and founded villages. According to their customs and traditions the Mundas, Hos, Santals and the like governed the societies through their own panchayats. Traditionally if there was an excessive population in a village, some of the villagers would select another suitable place for their habitation on an auspicious day. We can quote a Santal song to relate how a new village was founded :-

takay mae chiyalet bir disam do,
takay mae doramlet sagun ma thili
Marang Burui chiyalet bir disam do
Jaher Eray daramlet sagun ma thili.
Who chose the forest land and
who placed the holy earthen pitcher
Marang Buru chose the forest land and
Jaher Era placed the holy earthen pitcher.

The whole villagers worked unitedly to bring peace and prosperity to the village. The land and forests were the main sources of tribal economy. At the village level, the tribal social institutions regulated the right of the use of land and forest.

Community consensus emanating from village functionaries guided the tribal social life. Thus tribal social life was both democratic and open. Their social institutions regulated all aspects of life from *janam* to *gujuk* i.e. birth to death. According to tribal tradition at the end of the year in *Magh*, all village functionaries voluntarily resigned their posts. The idea was to subject their performances to social evaluation. Accordingly if there was anything wrong with the village functionaries, they had to take fresh mandate. At the same time each village household relinquished its right to the use of land allotted to it. All village lands were then redistributed according to the members of the family (Horkoren).

Village functionaries could maintain no secrecy in functioning. The deliberations were always open and every body had to voice his/her grievances. Nobody enjoyed any special prerogative. According to tribal thinking they are the product of the nature. They have reclaimed forest lands with hard labour. They have every right on reclaimed land. In a Santali song collected by the historian Dr. Dhirendrea Nath Baskey –

Bir barge noa orak'kak' alang,
Raja Rani nonde alang kak' alang,
Rengec' jala do lang erer gidia',
Serma reyak' suklang bhunjao sukjanga
Here in this forest land we shall build our houses,
spend our days like a king and queen,
forget our weal and woe,
enjoy heavenly happiness.

This pristine and hallowed living did not continue for long. Distortions gradually followed with the introduction of monarchical ideas and the immigration of outsiders with non-egalitarian values. In Chotanagpur Munda dynasty was established with Phani Mukut Rai, an adopted son of Madra Munda, in 64 A.D. Originally the post of Maharaja was elected. For running the royal expenses the Mundas traditionally sent *najrana* (tribute) to him. But with the passage of time Mankis, Mundas and Pahans were subdued to Maharaja. Maharaja began to lead the life in royal splendour. Excessive taxes were imposed on the ryots. Rajas from outside began to send gifts like horses, shawls etc. to the Maharaja of Chotanagpur. Matrimonial relationship was also established with the Rajput dynasties outside. For the functioning of royal administration, people were brought from outside like Bihar, Madhya Pradesh etc. The Brahmins, instead of the Pahans, were appointed for performing religious rites like the worshipping of *Singbonga* and other social rituals. In this way the people, who were brought from outside as servants, became the Jagirdars and Thikadars (contractors). Tribal people became discontent. Realising the discontent of tribals, the Maharaja appointed Chatrik, Boraik, Rautias as soldiers. Traditional system was thus gradually eroded.

In subsequent years Chotanagpur witnessed tremendous changes. The first was that its remaining political isolation was further broken. Maharaja Man Singh, the administrator of Bihar and Bengal, invaded Chotanagpur in 1580. Khukra or Jharkhand became the feudatory state in 1585 when Shahbaj Khan sent a troop of soldiers against the Maharaja. During the reign of Aurangzeb, the Maharaja of Chotanagpur shifted his capital from Ranchi to Duisa. In 1765 the Moghul Emperor Shah Alam II gave the Diwani of Bengal, Bihar and Orissa to the East India Company. This brought Chotanagpur region under British rule exposing the land and people to more baneful influences. Since 1767 a large number of British infiltrations began in the area. Due to the Permanent Settlement of 1793 lands were gradually transformed into an exchangeable commodity, an idea which was against tribal ethos. Alien Zamindars began to purchase the tribal lands ousting the tribal chiefs and petty Zamindars. Land alienation and consequent pauperization of tribals were the results. Once Chotanagpur was regarded as secluded as Tibet to outsiders but the land was gradually converted into the land for supplying coolies to tea gardens and collieries. Migration resulted not only in physical distress but it also affected the moral basis of their life.

In the year 1906 the Santals of Midnapur sent a petition to the Government through Rev. A.L. Kennen complaining against the loss of their land and consequent migration. The effect of the supply of labour is summed up as follows by the Rev. A.L. Kennen –

> 'Thousands of them, having become landless, wander the country seeking coolie work. The mingling of the sexes on the road, the miserable provision for their sleeping where they chance to labour, being herded together here and there amongst constantly changing companions without any of the restraint of the village organisation to which they have been accustomed, is rapidly lowering the morals of the community. Moreover this wandering life rapidly destroys any inclination they have towards patient industry. It is a feast or a famine. It lessens their love for home. It tends to increase petty wayside thefts and crimes. The mortality amongst these wanderers is very great, and greater amongst

infants and children who perish for diseases due to exposure. Those who retain their lands are still under a cloud. No one knows how soon he may be dispossessed. The encouragement to improve is absent. The better a man's land is, the sooner some Bengali will covet it and oust him from it'.(McAlpin, 1981)

In 1845 the Christian Missionaries started working in Chotanagpur region. They were able to convert some of the tribal people of the land because the tribals were also trying to get rid of the oppression of the alien Zamindars and Thikadars. According to S.P. Sinha 'The tribals of Chotanagpur were attracted towards them only on their (missionaries) assured help to fight alien Thikadars and Jagirdars. The tribals had little to do with the spiritual tenets of the Christianity or the Kingdom of Heaven. Converted tribal Christians got ample help from missionaries in regard to education, medical facilities, etc. but the missionaries were able to disintegrate the tribal Christians from their original societies and customs. It was because Christians in general had apathy towards original tribal moral values and moral consciousness'.

Nature, environment and ecology play the most important role in tribal life. They have developed their religious beliefs and practices around their life giving forces. The social festivals are based on agriculture, life is based on nature. They have established a symbiotic relationship with nature. They have built up their social, economic and religious lives around nature. Year starts with flower festival, ends with fruit festival. Still now a *tut'*, *cere/tut* bird informs them that the earth is revolving : –

Hesak' ma chatere ja gonsae tude doe rage kan,
bare ma lawerre ja gonsae gotrot' me doe sahet' kan
des cha nachuren ja gonsae disam cha bihuren,
nachurte ha nachuren ja gonsae gonsae des cha naturen
bihurte ha bihuren ja gonsae des cha bihuren.

'On the to top of pipal tree *tut* is calling, on the bending banyan twig the *gotrot'* is taking its long breathe of relief. Oh God, the earth is revolving and revolving'. It suggests that according to the change of nature tribal mentality also changes.

Tribals take education from nature. They learn how their agricultural seasons have to be timed. To quote from a recent study – 'There are also many other plants which indicate the approach of the season or the correct time for certain activities e.g. when the *Sekrai* flowers blossom, gondli will be sown, as it is considered to be the right time for sowing. Another example is a particular type of rice known as '*hamal baba*' produced in bera land will be sown when *janum* (Jack) fruit is about to ripe, i.e., in June. Thus appearance of certain flowers or fruits indicate the time when certain activities should be carried out' (Bulletin, January 1961).

Unfortunately however the tribals were not allowed an undisturbed living in close proximity with natural surroundings. During British rule Forest Laws were promulgated, which prevented the tribals from reclaiming the forest lands and collecting forest products, an important item of their livelihood. This adversely affected them materially. Hence they were forced to enter into the larger labour market and come closer to the other groups of people. A socio-philosophical change in tribal life began to take place. In olden times, the Santals did not know the art of trickery and talking lies. To substantiate I would like to quote from Guru Kolean's *Horkoren Mare Hapramko Reak' Katha* –

> *'pahil do hor hopon ere phasiara katha do bale roret' tahekana, neko saheb hopon then khonge ere phasiara katha dole cet' akat'a . Ona katha do nonka lekatele cet' akada ban'ma bakea birre Sido Kanhoko sap' ket' kina. Ado jhilimili bangla then agukate ko phasiket' kina ar unkin songeren hor ho ko girip dar agulet' koa, ado unre sahebe kuliyet koa – am hom khunakada – horemgoe' akat' koa, ado unreko angue' got'leda – hen goe' akatkoa. Ado onkage dher hore phasiket' ko khange – saheb do caprasiye metat' koa – do noko hordo lai akope jemon ereko ror ar bankhan tinak'bo phasikoa. Ado caprasi do onko khunahi hor then sen kateko menkeda – ape don laiapekana saheb nahak' kulipe jokhen tinrey metapea – am horen goe' akat' koa – unre metaepe in do ban goe akat'koa ado mahakpe bancaok'aohoe phasipea. Ado sari pe pon hor onkako bancaoen khan ina kathage joto horko capetente ko rorkeda khangeko bancaoena. Ado unre*

> *hor hoponko menkeda – dureya noa do ere halop kana cekate endekhan hor ko bancaoena, ado un khonge ere phasiara kathado hor hopon talare boloakanaedo nitkotedo barti hor hopon lar careda arko bhajaueda ere kathate ho muhim khon pakrom kangea'(Horkoren).*

'In ancient times we the Santals were not accustomed in giving deceitful statement and talking lies, we learnt to talk a lie from the European. When Sido, Kanhu were arrested in the Bakea forest then they were taken to Jhilimili bungalow and were hanged to death. Their followers were also arrested and were taken to that bungalow. The Englishman enquired one of the arrested persons – 'have you committed murder?' The arrested person replied – 'Yes I have committed murder'. He was also hanged to death. The other person was also enquired, he also confessed and was hanged to death. Then the Englishman summoned his servant, go and tell the arrested persons to give false statement – we shall hang how many people. The servant went to them and told – I telling you that when the Englishman will ask you – have you committed murder, then you will tell him – I have not committed murder, then you will be saved. Then three-four persons were saved and rest of people said alike and were saved. Then the Santals told among themselves – if we gave false statements then how we could be saved. From then only, the habit of talking lies introduced in the Santal Society and till now many Santals are in a habit of talking lies and in such fraudulent ways many are in a position to overcome their difficulties'.

In her article entitled 'The Hos of Saranda: An Ethnographic Study' Rekha O Dhan stated

> 'the Mankis and the Mundas, conscious of their social and political power have begun to misuse their power. The method of settling disputes is not very satisfactory, as the disputes are made subject of retaliation or of private gain and private grudges are satisfied by deliberately manipulating evidence. From their associations with the Dikus, they have many vices, with the result that most of them are dishonest, grabbing and quarrelsome. There have been many cases of embezzlement, bribery and corruption. They are no longer dependent for their position on the good

will of the people, because they are dependent more on the administration and they please the officers, rather than the people. Consequently, the village panchayat has lost control over them. To add to this emigration of labour to the mining areas and the flow of alien elements of the Dikus who have come to live among them, all these have resulted into the general distrust of the efficacy of the established mores, customs, traditions and institutions. Thus the outside contact and the resulting complexities of life in general have made people to underestimate the importance of tribal laws. Today incest is not punished by murder. In olden days incest was considered to be the most serious offence and the offender was made to realize the guilt and to redress the wrong committed by him by offerings and sacrifices before the whole village. Today the offender may even escape punishment. Thus the offender may not feel guilty at all. Consequently more and more people are encouraged to disobey the tribal laws and to omit the performance of customary rights and rituals'. (Bulletin, 1961)

With the above distortions which had their origin during colonial rule, tribal life had to face a cultural crisis which has intensified in recent years. After the entry of Christianity, the Christian Santal elites have been trying to assume the leadership of the entire Santal population, Munda or Ho population, though they have totally forgotten the tribal identity markers. As against this the elites of *Jetke Santals* (*Jetke* is the term derisively used by Christian Santals for the non-Christian Santals), who some fifty years ago were in minority among the elites but have now developed enough collective consciousness, pose a challenge to Christian Santal leadership. As a result we find a very interesting power clash between the Santal elites and the Church .The next crisis originates in conflicting attitude towards Hinduism. While the non-Christian Santal elites, with the combination of other Kherwar peoples like Mahli, Kurmi, Hor, Dom, Penre etc., try to resist the Brahmanical caste-based domination and the Diku onslaught, another section is falling a prey to the ideology preached by the R.S.S. and business communities. Thereby a kind of communalism has been developed by different forces. Moreover, with the inclusion of political leaders in West Bengal

Santal Language Commission, the philosophical aspects of the language movement have been subordinated to political ideology.

The cumulative impact of the above forces is very disruptive. The fundamentalism-guided ethnocentricism has succeeded in dividing the *Hor-Mitan* solidarity, thereby posing a threat to collective-value-based *Hor-Mitan* social civilization. There is a growing tendency among the Santal boys and girls to incorporate non-tribal cultural idioms like Saraswati and Durga puja as well as other Hindu festivals. The tribal elites are found less attentive to their own dance and music, the dress and clothing, food and drinks. The folktales, myths and legends of the tribals are not the instrument of socialization in school and college education. As a result their entire worldview has been pushed to the background in the man making process in entire eastern India. Thus a cultural silence or *Nirbakization* has been developed within the tribals. They have been reduced into mere human cattle to serve the policies of globalization, privatization and liberalization.

References

Baskey, D.N. *Saontal Ganasangramer Itihas*, Pearl Publishers, Calcutta, 1982.

Bulletin of the Bihar Tribal Research Institute,Vol. III, No. I, January, 1961, The Bihar Tribal Research Institute, Ranchi.

For an English translation of Horkoren see P. O. Bodding, *Traditions and Institutions of the Santhals,* Bahumukhi Prakashan, New Delhi, 1994.

'Hor Hoponak Sedae Katha' published by the Santali Academy in 1996.

Hunter, W.W. *The Annals of Rural Bengal,* Cosmo Publications, Delhi, 1975.

McAlpin, M.C. *Report on the Condition of the Sonthals in the District of Birbhum, Bankura, Midnapore and North Balasore,* Calcutta, 1981.

Roy, S.C. *The Mundas and their Country,* Asia Publishing House, Calcutta, 1970.

Sinha, S.P. *Life and Times of Birsa Bhagwan,* Bihar Tribal Research Institute, Ranchi, 1964.

4

Eternal and Ephemeral
The Significance of Myth and Ritual among the Ho

Ritambhara Hebbar

The paper presents a series of origin myths, which are a few of the many that I came across among the Ho during my stay in West Singhbhum.[1] The attempt is to understand the underlying meanings of these myths and explain their significance in the lives of the Ho. I argue that these myths not only form the intellectual reservoirs of the Ho, but also provide an insight into Ho philosophy regarding their relationship with the supernatural and the natural world. I seek to demonstrate how the morals of the myths are enacted and committed to memory in *Maghe Parab,* the main festival of the Ho celebrated between the months of January and March to mark the beginning of a new agricultural cycle, in order to establish a symbiotic relationship between spirits, humans and the natural world.

Creation or origin myths of different cultures of the world stand in direct contrast to the scientific theory on the origin of the earth and, by that count, would be dismissed as *untrue* and *illusory* accounts of phenomena incomprehensible by so called 'primitive people'.[2] More often than not, the quintessence of origin myths are lost out in a never-ending debate about whether the events as described in myths ever happened at all. Therefore, it is necessary that I state at the outset itself that this paper is not about the debate on the relationship of stories of origins with fiction or truth. Nonetheless, to overcome this essential problem in the study of myths, I would like to quote an excerpt from Marx's *Economic and Political Manuscripts of 1844,* which would allow us to isolate the problem with the popular understanding of origin myths and rephrase the question of origins anew in order to proceed in our enquiry on the role of myths in the lives of the Ho (1977 [1959]: 106-8).

The creation of *earth* has received a mighty blow from *geognosy*—i.e., from the science which presents the formation of the earth, the development of the earth, as a process, as a self-generation...

Now it is certainly easy to say to the single individual what Aristotle has already said: *You have been begotten by your father and your mother; therefore in you the mating of two human beings--a species-act of human beings--has produced the human being. You see, therefore, even physically man owes his existence to man. Therefore you must not only keep sight of the one aspect—the infinite progression which leads you further to inquire: Who begot my father? Who his grandfather? Etc. you must also hold on to the circular movement sensuously perceptible in that progress by which man repeats himself in procreation, man thus always remaining the subject. You will reply, however: I grant you this circular movement; now grant me the progress which drives me even further until I ask: who begot the first man, and nature as a whole? I can only answer you: Your question itself is a product of abstraction. Ask yourself how you arrived at that question. Ask yourself whether your question is not posed from a standpoint to which I cannot reply, because it is wrongly put. Ask yourself whether that progress as such exists for a reasonable mind. When you ask about the creation of nature and man, you are abstracting, in so doing, from man and nature. You postulate them as non-existent, and yet want me to prove them to you as existing. Now I say to you: Give up your abstraction and you will also give up your question. Or if you want to hold on to your abstraction, then be consistent, and if you think of man and nature as non-existent, then think of yourself as non-existent, for you too are surely nature and man...Or are you such an egoist that you can conceive everything as nothing, and yet want yourself to exist?*

You can reply: I do not want to postulate the nothingness of nature, etc. I ask you about its genesis, just as I ask the anatomist about the formation of bones, etc.

But since for the socialist man the *entire so-called history of the world* is nothing but the creation of man through human labour, nothing but the emergence of nature for man, so he has the visible, irrefutable proof of his *birth* through himself, of his *genesis*. Since the real existence of man and nature has become evident in practice, through sense experience, because man has thus become evident for man as the being of nature, and nature for man as a the being of man, the question about the *alien* being, about a being above nature and man—has become impossible in practice.

Thus the 'truth-value' of the story of origin does not lie in the denial of the 'mediation' of God in it and getting entangled in an enquiry on who begot the first human in order to ascertain our origins, as it would only lead us to a dead end. Not only would this form of questioning be human-centric, but also restrictive, in that it negates the role of nature and thereby unwittingly puts into question our own existence. It assumes a point of beginning, from where all things grew and developed and recognizes one by denying role of another. In fact, this form of questioning is as conjectural as what it contests. The real question that stories of origin answer, therefore, is not as to *who* created the universe, but *how* was it created, as the latter allows us to proceed from the here and now, the present and that which is at hand. The answer to the question on how the earth came into being would always lead the questioner to examine the realm of practice. It is in the routines and traditions associated with earth that provide the justification for stories of origin just as the origin myths provide the bases for their existence. In other words, it gives us an insight into the philosophical underpinnings that orient everyday life and practices. It is this relationship between myth, ritual and practice that I seek to unravel in the context of the Ho tribe. I refer to the myths of origin and the *Maghe Parab* ritual, as it is practiced in Mirra, a village in West Singhbhum.[3]

Creation Myths

Here are some of the Myths as narrated in the village :

The boundary between spirits and humans was set at the time of creation. At the time of creation, there was water all around. There was no life and this disturbed the sun and the moon. The moon decided to hide her two children, a boy and a girl in a crab and left the crab in the water. Having saved her two children, she wondered as to how they would survive in the water. So the sun and the moon decided to create an earthworm, which defecates earth. Gradually, the earthworm filled the water with earth. Places where the earthworm defecated more became hillocks and the rest is either plain land or water. We are on water; earth is on top of water.

Before man settled in villages and at the time when earth had just come into being, man would live in the jungle. There was no division between the world of god, man and animals. Man could see and speak with god and animals. Rice used to grow un-husked in the plain fields. This changed with time. Man can no longer see and speak with god and animals and nor does rice grow un-husked.

It happened like this. Once a group of men performed a ritual in the name of the supreme spirit of the Ho, *Singbonga* and sacrificed a cock. After the ritual was over, they forgot to take the knife, which was used for the sacrifice. Halfway through their journey they realized this and sent one of the men to collect it. On reaching the place, he saw *Singbonga,* their God, licking blood off the ground. He asked God, ' *Singbonga,* why are you licking the blood when you can have the meat instead'? God was taken by surprise and said, 'Oh, you have seen me licking blood off the ground. All right, in future you will not be able to see me'. He applied the juice of *soso* seeds (seeds of the marking nut tree, which on being rubbed on any part of the body leaves a mark) on the man's eyes. His eyes became black. This is the reason why the portion around man's eyes is black. Since that day man cannot see or speak with God.

Rice grains grew unhusked in the open fields. Man did not respect God's creation and misused the favour that God had granted him. He would pluck and eat it while defecating in the field. God was annoyed by this act of man and decided that from then on rice grains would grow husked.

The following incident occurred when man had just started cultivating land. Man took his oxen to plough land. After a while the oxen got tired and said, 'Master, feed us and then we can start work again'. To this man replied, 'Work for a little while more and then I will feed you'. A few hours later the oxen repeated their request. This happened three to four times. Finally, the oxen got exhausted and disgusted with their master's behaviour. They swore not to speak with man ever again. Similarly, the story behind the Gopes taking up the livelihood of cattle tending is as follows. Once there was a *Gope,* an *Adivasi,* God and his servant. God asked the Gope to inform cattle that, from that day on, they should eat one day and bathe every day. The Gope communicated the opposite, that is, that they should eat all days and bathe one day. On hearing of the mistake committed by the Gope, God gave the responsibility of feeding and taking care of cattle to the Gope.

Among animals, the tiger is more powerful as compared to the ox. This is so because of an unequal distribution of strength between animals. The story is as follows:

...When God was distributing strength, the ox went up to God and complained, "You have given me the task of feeding humans, but I do not have enough strength to fulfil my duty". God decided to grant him more strength and asked him to come later in the day to collect an additional portion of strength. A tiger, which was hiding behind a bush and listening to the conversation, decided to get the portion of strength for himself. He came a few minutes before the ox and yelled out to God for the portion. God mistook the tiger for the ox and threw the portion towards him. The tiger quietly ate up the portion all by himself and slinked out of the place before the ox could see him. After a while, the ox came to collect the portion of strength and called out to God. On hearing the ox, God wondered as to what the ox could want again and said, "You came minutes ago, what do you want from me now"? The ox was taken aback by God's retort and explained that he had come just then and had got delayed on the way. To this God replied, "Fine then, since your portion has been eaten up by another animal, I will scrape out the left over for you...you can have that". The ox had to satisfy himself of the little that God gave him.

Thus, the undifferentiated expanse of water was covered by earth, which transformed the latter with a landscape distinguishable by its varied vegetation and diverse life forms. God, humans and animal at the time of creation could see and speak with each other. They shared a common language. This gave a semblance of equality to their relationship making it difficult to distinguish the boundaries of each. Man overstepped his boundary and began interfering in the work of God. It encouraged a sense of complacency in man about God's presence and his creation. The transition from the growth of un-husked rice to husked rice took place to instill a sense of respect in man for the work of God, which could be possible only through the intervention of human labour. Communication between God and man was no longer through speech, but through human labour. Human labour thus complemented the work of God in the reproduction of nature. On the other hand, the oxen substituted speech with labour and reconciled to their fate as subservient to man. The worlds of God, human and animal were set apart, distinguishable from each other.

The recurring themes of these myths are forgetfulness, memory lapses, misunderstanding, impudence, carelessness and indiscretion. Humans had to pay a price for their lack of discretion with God's creation. The ox had to settle with less strength because of his own doing or fault and the Gope lost out on a better alternative because of a misunderstanding. According to Levi-Strauss (1985: 191),

...the motif of forgetfulness as it appears in myths signals a failure to communicate with oneself, and if, in very different societies and eras, this motif is used mainly to lay the foundation of ritual practices, then the true function of ritual is, as I have suggested elsewhere...to preserve the continuity of experience. For it is this continuity that forgetfulness breaks on a mental level: we recognize this process when we speak of a memory lapse.

Thus myths are reminders of the 'memory lapse' or the forgetfulness at the time of creation. They serve as justifications for practice, of things as they are, as well as why things came to be the way they are. In this sense, practice revises the 'faux pas' committed at the time of creation and, in so doing, it is not an attempt at forgetting but preserving the memory of the 'faux pas'. Rituals are the media through which the memory of the 'faux pas' is played out in practice. Rituals therefore mediate between practice or everyday life and myth, in that they, as Bourdieu argues, can be grasped only in action and are temporal and yet detemporalize the everyday to refer to a mythico-ritual space. The 'ritual praxis', as Bourdieu calls this ambivalence associated with rituals, then 'enacts, in the form of real actions, that is, body movements, the operations that theoretical analysis discovers in mythic discourse, an opus operatum that masks the constituting moment of "mythopoeic" practice under its reified significations' (Bourdieu 1990: 93). The ritual associated with *Maghe Parab* is a case in point of the constituting moment of mythopoeic practice, in that not only does the ritual enact the 'faux pas' of the mythic experience, but also invokes its resolution of setting apart the world of humans, nature and the spirit world. The ritual thus preserves the continuity of the mythic experience and in doing so resets the grounds for constituting a 'home' in the forest, which would be impossible without appeasing and pacifying the spirit world.

Maghe Parab Ritual and the Mythic Reconciliation

The entire village celebrates *Maghe Parab* collectively. The ritual is an invocation to the *bonga ko seemana,* or the boundary of spirits, which in Ho villages forms the circumference of the village often separating the village from the forest and the villagers from the spirit world. In this sense, this boundary is both corporeal and cosmic, in that it is a physical marker of the cosmic distance between the world of humans from that of spirits and nature. The ritual therefore invokes the cosmic in its corporal manifestation, with references to its abode in the forest and at the limits of the village. It is this interconnectedness of the natural world with the spirit world, which distinguishes Ho philosophy towards their natural habitat from modern scientific understanding of forests as 'resource' or 'matter' valuable only for its material worth and allows for a humbler relationship vis-à-vis the natural world. The celebration of *Maghe Parab* is a collective evocation of the relationship with the forest and the spirit world.

The *deori* or the priest who performs the ritual takes a dip in the pond in the jungle, washes the freshly harvested *Biri* (a pulse) and returns to his house. From there again, the procession follows him to the *Desauli* or the sacred grove.[4] The *deori* carries with him *Biri* paste, rice, turmeric, while people along with him carry a cock, a hen and a chicken. The *deori* faces the *Desauli* and selects a spot for performing the ceremony. He then cleans the place with cow dung. Having done so, he makes two rows with twelve columns on the ground. He puts turmeric in the two corners of the upper columns and rice in the rest of the upper columns. In the lower columns, he puts *biri. Biri* is the chief crop of the upland, while rice is the main crop of the *Bera* land.[5] He then places *lamai* seeds on the columns with rice and sprinkles vermilion over it. The villagers use *lamai* leaves to make *poo* or leaf-cups. The leaves are shaped like a heart and give the impression of two halves of leaves joint together. Both turmeric and vermilion are considered as auspicious and used in most rituals in the village. In fact, vermilion is an essential medium of divination, through which the diviner discerns the presence of spirits in cases of sorcery and witchcraft. The *deori* smears the *biri* paste over his forehead, forearms, and places it on his ankles and behind his ear like an ornament.

Some of the people standing near the *deori* beat the drums, while some dance to its beat. A number of villagers hurl abuses randomly, as the *deori* recites the invocation. The term *'maghe'* in Ho is associated with dirty or obscene language. And it is on the occasion of *Maghe Parab* that *maghe kaji* or talk is a ritual exigency. According to the villagers, bad language is a means to excite the cock and the hen so that when they are sacrificed, the blood gushes out with force to spill over the ritual site. The latter is read as a sign of a good monsoon. At the end of the ritual, a yellow flower and grass is tied to the feathers of the chicken and thrown into the air. The villagers throw stones at it and the person who manages to strike it down is blessed in the coming year with a good season of hunting in the jungle. Fresh wood, leaves are cut and collected to carry the hen, cock and the chicken to the *deori's* house, thereby also enacting a return from a good hunt.

On *Maghe Parab,* nobody is supposed to take offense of the public disavowal of a sense of propriety, or the breach of codes of social conduct. Interestingly, the word *maghe* is made of two syllables: *Ma* and *Ge*. *Ma* is an enclitic, similar to the word do in English. *Ma* also means to cut, slash, chop with a swinging motion, e.g., *ma : bandi* (to cut off the head of a goat) or ma: gur (to cut down a tree or to make it fall). *Ge* like *Ma* is an enclitic, but also means a man's sister's child or a woman's brother's child. Given the practice of cross cousin marriage among the Ho, both (mother's brother's daughter and father's sister's son) are potential alliances for a prospective bridegroom. *Maghe* in this sense would suggest breaking off with affines, or giving up the good manners, decorum that accompanies interaction with affines. *Maghe Parab* is the festival that inverts the social structure only to establish it anew through the ritual. But, more importantly, it is a ritual enactment of the impudence, derision and irreverence characteristic of the mythic experience, as demonstrated through the complete flippancy associated with norms, customs in relation to affines and sexual conduct, which in actual practice is met with scorn and contempt. Similarly, the hurling of abuses at the *deori* is the ritual performance of the mythic transgression whereby humans mistook divine benevolence for their prerogative and right.

In the invocation of the ritual, prayers are offered to all the spirits of the village. The spirits of the village are invoked in the ritual, through mimetic actions of good rains and hunting in the forest as illustrated above, to bless the villagers with a year of plenty, of good monsoons and harvests, health and safety of the villagers and their livestock and to protect them of evil spirits. The villagers also express their veneration and gratefulness to the spirit world for their kindness and benevolence through the previous year. There is then, along with the enactment of the mythic experience, an acknowledgement of the 'faux pas' and a simultaneous revision of the same in the ritual. Therefore, through the *Maghe Parab* ritual, there is a corporeal as well as a cosmic reconciliation of the mythic experience of transgression and disrespect in relation to the spirit and the natural world.

References

Bourdieu, Pierre. 1990. *The Logic of Practice. Stanford*: Stanford University Press.

Deeney, J., s.j. 1978. *Ho Grammar and Vocabulary*. Chaibasa: Xavier Ho Publications, St Xavier's High School.

Levi-Strauss, Claude. 1985. *The View From Afar. United Kingdom*: Basic Baswell Books.

Marx. Karl. 1977. *Economic and Political Manuscripts of 1844*. Moscow: Progress Publishers.

Notes

1. I conducted my Ph. D fieldwork in West Singhbhum between May, 1996 and July, 1998. My Ph. D research is titled 'Ho and their Environment: A Case Study of West Singhbhum District'.
2. This was the dominant view in the 19th and the first half of the 20th century regarding subjective association of nature with spirits and divinities. This subjectivity vis-à-vis the natural world was considered it to be an impediment to human's control over the natural environment and to the spread of modern science. These explained the inability of peoples with such beliefs to exploit nature for their advantage and were broadly categorized as 'primitive' and 'backward'.
3. Mirra village is located in the south of West Singhbhum and is surrounded by a Protected Forest Block. The forests have been and still are integral to the lives of the villagers. It is for this reason that *Maghe Parab* ritual retains its original significance and meaning for the villagers as well as for research on the relationship of the Ho with their natural and spirit world.
4. Every Ho village has at least one sacred grove in the village, which is the resting place of the village spirit. All collective village rituals are performed in the *Desauli*.
5. *Bera* lands are lands that hold moisture for the longest period of time and are most suitable for rice cultivation.

5

Changing World Views of the Indigenous (Mulvasi-Adivasi) People of Jharkhand
A Socio-Philosophical Perspective

Pashupati Prasad Mahato

Introduction

The anthropological study of changing worldview is in fact in a state of stagnation in Indian situation. I doubt if it could be set going again by making minor alterations in classical theoretical themes. According to Greetz (1966) four contributions of the man, i.e. Durkheim's discussion of the nature of the sacred, Weber's Verstehenden methodology, Freud's parallel between personal rituals and collective one's, and Malinowski's exploration of the distinction between regional and common sense are inevitable starting points for any useful anthropological theory of religion or philosophy of life. To a student of social Anthropology, it denotes an historically transmitted pattern of meanings, embodied in symbols, a system of inherited conceptions expressed in symbolic forms by means of which men communicate, perpetuate and develop their knowledge about and attitudes towards life. The sacred symbols and aesthetics towards life function to synthesize a people's ethos, resulting in the difference between taboos and profane. Thus the tone, character and quality of life, its moral and aesthetic values and style, the mood and the expressive language encompass the worldview of the people. But I fear that the above four dominating ideas instead of advancing our knowledge parochialize it.

In religious belief and practices a group's ethos is rendered intellectually reasonable by being shown to represent a way of life ideally adapted to the actual state of affairs the worldview describes. The worldview is rendered emotionally convincing by being presented as an image of an actual state of affairs peculiarly well arranged to accommodate such a way of life. So the famous definition of Tylor–'the belief in spiritual beings' is not fitting with the modern anthropological studies. The present day social-science-studies consider worldviews as a cultural system, which is not only a parameter to understand man and man relationship but is also a significant tool to understand man and nature (bio-diversity), man and supernatural relationships.

The present paper takes up the changing worldview of Jharkhand tribals. It starts by projecting the spatio-demographic ambience. It also seeks to highlight the strong cultural bias of so called civilized people against the indigenes. The second section questions the very principle of scheduling some people as tribe and argues the inclusion of some others in the list of scheduled tribes. The last takes up tribal aesthetics as reflected in their spatio-centric worldview.

The term *Jharikhand* or Jharkhand, which I am using here, is the area termed by 'Jahangir Nama', a Mughal chronicle, using ancient Sanskrit texts. Prof. D.D. Kosambi termed the whole forest tract as *Atavika Rajya*. We get its reference in Prof. Irfan Habib's famous book *An Atlas of the Mughal Empire* in the 16th century. The biographer of Shri Chaitanya Mahaprabhu, in his famous Bengali verse *Chaitanya Charitamrita*, referred the term *Jharikhand.* This vast forest tract is at present under different states of Indian Union, namely Orissa, West Bengal, Chattisgarh, Jharkhand and Bihar. Though on 15 November, 2000, a separate province known as Jharkhand has been carved out from Bihar, yet the term Jharikhand still remains valid more as a single ecological and cultural unit.

Besides spatial the land had since ages a demographic uniqueness also. The ethnic groups, who lived here as indigenous people, were termed in the Brahmical Sanskrit texts, scriptures and inscriptions as Savar/Sabar, Nishad, Pulinda, Rakshasa, Kol-villa, Dasyu, Das, Danav, Asur, Banar, Valluk and Kutumbin etc. The Aryan victors considered them as Anarya or non-Aryan or indigenous aborigines of India. Since the beginning of the Aryan colonization, cultural invasion and violence were perpetrated on these indigenes of eastern India.

The Kols formed an important element among the non-Aryans. About their mythological origin, S.C. Roy (1912) observed –

'Another ancient Sanskrit work gives still another fabulous account of the Kols – the generic name for the Mundas and other Kolarian Tribes. It tells us that Raja Bena having been tainted with sin, the Rishis went to remonstrate with him. The Raja with a wave of his hand beckoned the Rishis to depart. Thereupon the sage Angira cursed him, and, as a result of the curse, the offending right hand of the Raja was immediately converted into a churning stick. And from this arm sprang a man short in stature, black as the crow, with short arms, high cheek bones, small legs and flat nose, red eyes and tawny hair. This man became Nishada. When the Rishis began to churn the left hand of Bena, three more men came out of the arm the Mushahantara, the Kolla and the Villa – the first ancestors of the Mushahars, the Kols, the Bhills of our own days'.

It should however be noted that the aborigines of India do not register an autonomous presence in the Sanskrit literature. Roy informs that they make only passing references to the aborigines of India in order to glorify the victorious progress of the Aryan arms into the country. Occasionally however we hear of the humiliation of Aryan prowess at the hands of the hated Dasyus. Thus in the Sapta Sati, in the Chandi Path of the Markandeya Puran, we hear some pig-eating warriors of an unclean tribe defeating the Aryan King Surath of the Chaitra race.

Uncleanliness remains the lingering motif. The epithet 'कोला बिध्वंसिन:' slayers of pigs, i.e., pig eaters, in this passage has been supported by Herr Jelinghans and others to refer to the Kols or Kolarian tribes so called from their habit of eating pigs, which is considered unclean by the Aryans.

The other dominant idea was the beastliness and sub-humanness. According to Roy 'in the account of the Great War in the Mahabharata we hear Sanjaya in describing the arrangement of the Kaurava army name the Mundas with the Karushas, the Vikanjas, and the Kentibrishas, as forming the left wing commanded by Vrihadvala. Again, we hear the great Aryan warrior Satyaki comparing the Mundas to the Danavas or demons, whom he boasts - मुण्डानेतान हनिष्यामि दानवानिव वासव: (I shall kill these Mundas even as Indra killed the Danavas).

The first great epic, the Ramayana by Balmiki, expresses a grudge against the Nishads or the indigenous black people of India. Mahato (1998) thus remarked 'Since then the institutionalized and structural violence of discrimination and hatred was let loose to tame those people to generate surplus labour or human cattle for the Bhu-devatas or the Brahmins'. The Hindu mythology thus prejudices the mind of people against the most human and civilized people of India who are the indigenous people. Due to this bias, as Mahato (2000) points out even the beauty and grace of women like Putuna, Hidimba, Surpanakha, Chitrangada, etc of mythical origin were never treated at par with Subhadra, Kunti, Draupadi, Sita, Radha etc.

II

I now take up the question of the demography of Jharkhand. In this section I argue that the very definition of scheduled tribe, considered to be the indigenes, should be more broad-based so as to include some other people. But before taking up my argument I would like to dilate on the very meaning of the term tribe. The Report of ILO – Convention 1957 (No. 107), Geneva 1-10 September, 1986, meeting of the Experts on the Revision of the Indigenous and Tribal populations gave the working definition of the indigenous people, which reads as follows: – 'Indigenous communities, peoples and nations are those which, having a historical continuity with pre-invasion and pre-colonial societies that developed on their territories, consider themselves distinct from other sectors of the societies now prevailing in those territories or parts of them. They form at present non-dominant sectors of society and are determined to preserve, develop and transmit to future generations their ancestral territories and their ethnic identity as the basis of their continued existence as people, in accordance with their own cultural pattern, social institutions and legal systems'.

The meaning of scheduled tribe and *adivasi* is not uniform in wide academic perspective. Boas, a noted anthropologist, defined 'By tribe we usually mean an economically independent group or people speaking the same language and writing to defend themselves against outsiders'. On the other hand, Prof. D.N. Majumdar observed 'A tribe is a collection of families, group of families bearing a common name, members of which occupy the same territory, speak the same language and observe certain taboos regarding marriage, profession or occupation and have developed a well assessed system of reciprocity and mutuality of obligation'.

In Indian scenario, the word 'tribe' or adivasi had replaced the word indigene. I fear that the Indian ruling class–bureaucrats, politicians, media nexus are trying very systematically to convince Indian people that only scheduled tribes mentioned in the Article 341 of Indian Constitution are considered to be tribe or adivasi. The Government of India or the Constitution of India never gave any definition of the scheduled tribe, but said that the communities or ethnic groups enlisted in the Constitution by the order of the President of India is to be considered as scheduled tribe. But I would like to point out that the Indian Constitution also provided that the Parliament may by law include in or exclude people from the list of scheduled tribes.

In the above light I shall now seek to explore whether the list of scheduled tribes is really exhaustive in Indian situation. The criteria for judgment are the ones determined by the Lakur Committee (1965). These are: indications of primitive traits, distinctive culture, geographic isolation, shyness of contact with community at large and backwardness.

In eastern India many small and numerically large demographic groups are yet not considered tribes. Ashok Kumar Mahato (2002) observed 'In the history of peasantry, the Kutumbins occupy an important role as a peasant class of ancient India. In the Arthashastra of Kautilya (2.4) they were mentioned as sharecroppers. According to the prescription of Kautilya the Superintendent of Agriculture (Sitadhyaksa) shall employ slaves, labourers, and prisoners to sow the seeds on the well-ploughed lands of the king. In the commentary of Arthashastra, T. Ganapati Shastri mentions two sorts of slaves namely udardasa and kritadasa. The assistants to supply the agricultural implements were the blacksmiths, carpenters, borers, rope makers, those who catch snakes and such other persons of same kind. All the people mentioned above are grouped into Sudra class and the untouchables of the society. So it may be considered that the Kutumbins who were assisted by the helping hands such as the blacksmiths, carpenters, etc. were also to be included both in the classes of the Sudra and the untouchables'.

While analyzing the *'Goun-Ghar'* system of the Kudmis of Jharkhand, I (2002) have observed that the same reciprocity and obligation in sharing the marriage and death, childbirth including the production of the paddy is found among them. All the cross sections of the people related to the production are invited in marriage, death, and childbirth of the Kudmi-Mahatos. They are the Dom (drummer), the Hari (placenta cutting women), the Ful or Saiha or Sangat or the ceremonial friends, the basket makers, the Dom or Mahli, the blacksmith or Kamar, the Pan, Baraik, Chick Baraik or Tanti, the weaver, Ghasi, Pytkar (scroll painter), Thetri (metal ornaments makers), the Malhars (metal lamp makers), the Jolha-Momins in Jharkhand and others. During these occasions the village headman the Manki, Munda, Mahato, Majhi were respected first with traditional gaiety and rituals.

What I seek to insist is the very notion of extended family, which includes the entire village community itself, found among Gour-Gope, Deswali-Majhi, Kudmi-Mahatos, Pytkar, Thethri, Karga, Pahadiyas etc. This is similar to the tribal trait still shared by many indigenous people of Eastern India, specially in Jharikhand like Santal, Munda, Oraon, Ho, Kharia, Asur, Bhumij, Korwa, Bijia etc. On the basis of this cultural similarity I believe that the above excluded groups of people should also be treated as indigenes and hence listed as scheduled tribes.

III

Besides the very notion of extended family among Jharkhandis I shall next highlight some of the specialities that outline the worldview of the indigenes. The traditional lyrics and collective creative excellences are reflected in their worldview in relation to their settlement (Janapada). In Ho language a wonderful lyric cum poetry, collected by a legal practitioner and noted historian of Chaibasa Sunil Kumar Sen and included in Dr. Sudhir Karan's book *Aranya Purush,* clearly reflects the imagination and emotional attachment to their wonderful land Singhbhum.

Nimin Bugin Disum eren janama kana
Angabira, Chariburu, Dalma-chutina singa,
sete bakai bewra kan
Sona Gara Samon Rakha, Bonga ko Gara Baitarini
Karo-Kuili Marang Garate Sajao Singara Kan.

'Our *Disum* is best among the all, encircled by the four hills, Angabira, Chariburu, Dalma-chutina are our lions seat. The Golden river Subarnarekha, the mighty Vaitarini and Koel and Karo, the divine deities abode in our land. The picturesque and beautiful is our land'.

The next is its very assimilative character. It shows that culturally adivasi worldview has been both receptive and recreative. A few centuries back the people of the vast tract of the Eastern India welcomed Vaishnavism. This influence inspired literary and artistic/ dance creations. As a result hundred and thousand love songs were composed in the model of Radha and Krishna

Jamuna Japare Sankhadaru Subare
Nida Singi go daigo rutui Navangtana
Dala buigo sabin len Jama.
Gara Gidil bedayana
Tiri riri Sadiyana
Ayumepe go daigo rutui...
Dala dala Sabin kuri
Dala buigo lele Juri
Ayu mepe go dai...

'In the riverbanks of Jamuna, from branches of Sankhadaru (Kadamba tree) the fruits' melodious sound is coming. Please do not go alone, otherwise you will not be in a position to come back. The melody is passing on the wave…'

Similarly a vast oral and written literature was developed in Kudmali, Mundari, Sadri and Nagpuria languages on the Vaisnav influence since the 17th Century. The poets like Binanandiya Singh, Budhu Babu, Gourangia Singh, Bhabaprita Nanda Ojha, Ramkrishna Ganguly, Khypa, Dina Tanti, Brajuram, Jagannath Mondal, Srishtidhar Mahato as well as the present composers like Dr. Ramdayal Munda, Bhabatosh Satpathy, Sunil Mahato, Krittibas Karmakar etc. emerged within last four hundred years.

The melody and rhythmic flurry, the ecstasy and superbly blended aesthetics feature the cultural life of the indigenous and tribal people in Jharikhand. It is marked by some unique folk dances in the region, namely the *Nachni Nach, Natua Nach, Danr Nach,* Karma and Sarhul dance, *Kirtan* dance and finally the *Chho* dance of the region, which is now acclaimed as one of the most vigorous and graceful dance forms of the world. This *Chho* dance in eastern India, especially in West Bengal, Orissa and Jharikhand is represented by (1) Manbhum school (2) Mayurbhanja school, (3) Saraikela school, (4) Kharsawan school and (5) Jhargram school.

The choreographers like Ruidas Mahato, Rajkishore Mahato, Lal Mahato, Jipa Sing Mura, Kalebar Kumbhar, Sudhir Kumbhar, Lal Mahato of Manbhum school; Subhendra Narayan Singhdeo and Mansukh Mahato of Saraikela school; Mangat Mahato of Mayurbhanja school etc. developed *Fut Nach* of the region, which is still prevalent in Jhargram sub-division of West Bengal.

Jharkhandi Nachni is one of the principal sources for highlighting the sportive activities of Srimati Radha and Krishna of Sri Chaitanya's Vaisnav cult. The Vaisnav professional narrators (*Kathak*) of scriptural and mythological stories had become tour mates of Sri Chaitanya Dev during his sojourn from Puri to Mathura. One purpose of this journey was to popularize the stories of Ramayan and Radha-Krishna sagas to the indigenous people. According to Sri Krishnadas Kabiraj, the writer of Sri Chaitanya Charitamrita –

"Jharikhander Patha Prabhu Karila Gaman Villa Praya Lok-Taha Param Pasanda."

'Lord has stepped out to the path of Jharikhanda, the people there are of adverse schooling, also extreme rustic'.

Here the word 'villa praya' signifies that at that time the worldviews of the indigenous people were completely different from the philosophy of Sri Chaitanya's Vaisnav cult. The indigenous people were then the worshippers of the Sun God or *Singbonga* and their religion centred round *Dhamma-Thakur*. So the nature worshipping (mainly trees, sun, moon, stones and hills) people were not initially very keen to accept the Vaisnav cult. That is why they have been termed as '*Pasanda*,' meaning cruel and ruthless people. Sri Chaitanya Dev temporarily resided in the villages of Gopiballavpur, Raghunathpur, Shyam-sundarpur, Jayadevpur, Krishnapur, Radhanagar etc. on the banks of Subarnarekha, Kangsabati, Vaitarini etc. He arranged for *Kathak* recital and dances to popularize the stories of Radha and Krishna to the locals through music. The local chieftains, talukdars and rajas were the hosts of Sri Chaitanya and his tour-mates.

As a result of these *Kathak* recitals and tunes *Srikrishna Kirtan* mingled with the local music and dance rhythms. The followers and disciples of Sri Chaitanya were extremely enthusiastic about synthesis. It is needless to say that there may be a great controversy about the fact that how much manifestation or adaptation has really taken place in today's *Nachni* dance or '*Kathak*' dance from the then '*Jharkhandi Kathak*'.

In his famous *Natya Sastra* or Drama Scriptures, sage/scholar Bharat (200 B.C. to 200 A.D.) had written about four main vocations – Acting, Dance, Singing and Music. He divided India chiefly into four main geographical fields, which he termed as '*Prabirti*'. These fields were *Avanti, Dakshinatya, Panchali* and *Odra-Magadhi*. His division of four vocations was later merged into two main vocations, which were known as '*Bharati*' and '*Kausiki*'. In *Kausiki* stream one notes the erotic songs, dance and music, while in '*Bharati*', the main stress is given to verbal dialogues with steps matching with these dialogues.

The oldest classical *Margi* stream of songs, dance and acting in India has exhausted itself fifteen hundred years back. In Jharkhand these two main streams of *Odra* and *Magadhi* can still be seen. The dance form of Jharkhand is famous by the name of *'Nachni'*. According to Abhinav Gupta (9th Century) the '*Bharati*' and *Kausiki* forms have mingled together and developed a new form known as *Nachni.* In this dance form the *Rasik* is eloquent with songs and acting amidst the dance. Later on mysticism and women counterparts, known as '*Sadhan Sangini'*, have also been incorporated. The philosophy of *Bindupatrod* or exercise to stop the semen discharge has been incorporated in *Sadhu* songs in Jharkhand and in other parts of Bengal. This *sadhana* is known as *Baul,* with the help of *Sahajiya* and *Sufi* saints in Jharkhand. Many lyrics were composed and the *Dehatatta* or philosophy of the anatomy of the male and female became centre point of the *Ekangi Sadhu, Jugalangi Sadhu* and *Bahulangi Sadhu.*

The development of *Chho* in Jharkhand is of very recent origin. Only it can go back to hundred forty to fifty years. But if we study the very stances and gaits of the dance we find that six local dance forms had been incorporated in *Chho* dance namely *Natua/Firkel/Fari Khanda* dance, a martial art of the region; *Nachni*, the dance form of *Lasya* or erotic; *Kirtan* or Vaisanav's mass prayer songs and dance; *Majhi Nach* or the dance of the Santals or Mundas or Hos of Jharkhand, which is a collective dance form of the male and females; *Danr Nach* or *Kathi Nach* of the Kudmi, Deswali, Gour or other indigenous people; and *Karam* dance a ritual dance of all the indigenous people of the entire Hor/Ho/Horo-Mitan people of Jharkhand. Mahato (1987) observes that the word *Chho* has nothing to do with *Chadma* or *Chhaya* (shadow) or *Chhauni* or military camp. It is the uniqueness of cultural collective excellence of the peasantry and artisans of Jharkhand who choreographed this world famous dance styles.

The collective reciprocity, assimilation and tolerance-based values with much more equality between man and woman found in the culture of Jharkhand had however to confront so called modernistic values found in courts, educational institutions and in work places. The simple adivasis are gradually lured into the individualistic, money minded and manipulating culture of the outsiders. Though both share the same geographical space for decades, adivasis have been forced for this basic difference in worldviews to treat them not as fellowmen but as *Dikus*.

I have no hesitation in agreeing with Elwin (1951) that the impact of so-called modern values has been disruptive for the indigenes of Jharkhand. An *adivasi* has been systemically encouraged 'to despise the teaching and achievements of his own tribe'. The modern education leads them to a world where tribal boys and girls are 'constricted to believe that all that is natural, open and simple is somehow bad'. Not moral distortion alone, tribal world today stands threatened before the so-called development projects, which do not hesitate to uproot them from their hearth and home.

In conclusion, I am pained to say that the most egalitarian, democratic, culturally literate people of this part of the country is collectively facing the culture of silence or *Nirbakization* caused by the continued process of cultural invasion and cultural violence of the so called civilized people. This has resulted in ethnic memocide of the indigenous/tribal people of the Eastern India. I insist that if any epistemic intervention is seriously initiated to appropriate knowledge academicians should be more receptive to what these simple people have to say about themselves and their world.

References

Geertz, Cliford, *Religion as Cultural System in Anthropological approaches to the study of Religion*. Edited by Michael Bentor. Tevistock Publication, 1966, London.

Ghatak, Niranjan, *The Scheduled Tribes of India in the New Millennium*. Read in the Seminar – Urgent Research in Anthropology in South-East Asia with special reference to India. Organized by Anthropological Survey of India, Kolkata, 2002.

Habib, Irfan, *An Atlas of the Mughal Empire*. Oxford University Press, Delhi, 1982.

Jharkhander Hor-Mitan (Kherowal) Samajik Savyata, Silpa Chetna O. Jiban Rasabhodh. Prasik. Durganagar, Kolkata, 2001.

Mahato, Ashok Kumar, The Ancient Indian Peasantry. The Kutumbins. Read in the Asiatic Society Seminar on Transformation and change among the indigenous people of Eastern India, 2002.

Mahato, P.P., *The Performing Arts of Jharkhand* B.B. Prakasan, Kolkata, 1987.

Mahato, P.P., Adivasi Arthaniti O. Bhumi Bybastha. B. B. Prakasan, Kolkata, 1987.

Mahato, P.P., *Jharkhander Hor-Mitan (Kherowal) Samajik Savyata, Silpa Chetna O. Jiban Rasabhodh.* Prasik. Durganagar, Kolkata, 2001.

Mahato, P.P., *Sanskritization vs Nirbakization a study of cultural silence and ethnic memocide in Jharkhand,* Sujan Publication, Kolkata, 2000.

Mahato, P.P., Surpanakha Theke Chunikotal in *Esho Mukto Karo,* edited by Maitraeyee Chattapadhyay. People's Book Society, Kolkata, 2000.

Roy, S. C., *The Mundas and their Country,* Calcutta, 1912.

6

Folk Treatment System of Tribal Society in Eastern India

Adikanda Mahanta

The word *adivasi* means the early settler or aboriginal. It implies that they have been residing in certain areas for longer period than others. So we can safely say that they are more experienced than those who entered these areas later.

Adivasis have been able to develop a folk tradition and culture drawing upon this rich experience. Yet the long gap, between the period it was supposedly made and the present, makes it sometimes illegible. It is applicable to all Indian tribes. Though the thought and philosophy of the *adivasi* influenced the Indian language, culture and philosophy in general yet accretions into it in course of time caused the departure of tribals themselves from their original philosophy. I would like to discuss it in the context of the medicine and method of treatment of the tribals in eastern India.

The districts of Orissa, Jharkhand, West Bengal, Assam, Bihar and Madhya Pradesh, where tribals live in large numbers, are surrounded by hills and dense forests. Education has not yet spread up to a reasonable extent of satisfaction. Moreover, there are poor communication facilities. This physical setting generally keeps them beyond the pale of so called modern allopathic system of medicine and inspires tribal people to have a strong faith in the use of the folk medicines available in the local areas.

The experts who use and apply the folk medicines, especially prepared from the plants, for the treatment of diseases, are commonly known as *Ojha* or *Ajha* – a rural doctor, but not a quack. This *Ojha* treats the patients in three different ways :

Medicinal method of treatment i.e. *Vesaja chikitsa paddhati*
Sound method of treatment i.e. *Sabda chikitsa paddhati*
Divine method of treatment i.e. *Daiba chikitsa paddhati*

The western educated person as well as the urban people may look down upon these *Ajhas,* as they are not so qualified in allopathic medicines. Even then their achievements are no less effective and significant compared to the achievements of the allopathic physicians. One obvious instance is that some chronic diseases, which are not cured by the allopathic medicines, can completely and easily be cured by the folk medicines. I shall next discuss the distinct features of different methods.

Vesaja Chikitsa Paddhati

The *Ajhas* give importance to the medicinal qualities of various plants, metals, stones and other substances derived from animals. They study the fluctuations of *Bata*, *Pitha* and *Khaph*, the three symptoms dissimilarly visible in diseased persons, and accordingly apply specific medicines. Sometimes some sort of counter-magic like *Tutuka* devised by the *Ojhas* are applied for treatment.

Moreover, the positions of the Sun, the Moon, the stars, the days and other astronomical bodies are given due consideration in the preparation and use of the medicines. These principles are widely applied through out eastern India. They also make use of medicinal plants found in almost all the forests of eastern India.

Sabda Chikitsa Paddhati

According to Hindu scriptures *Navi* – the abdomen is the centre of creation of sound. The sound created in this place is *Para Sabda* or *Nada Brahma.* The sound created in the upper portion of *Navi* is known as *Pashyanti Sabda.* From this place up to throat the sound created is known as *Madhyama Sabda* and from throat to mouth the sound created is known as *Baikhari Sabda.* Hindu scriptures hold that when produced in the right manners these sounds can cure diseases. This method of treatment has been devised by the Indians and remains confined to India. The other name of this sound measure of treatment is counter-magic method of treatment commonly known as *Mantra Chikitsa.* Though a western-educated person may disbelieve, a proper *Mantra Sadhak* or a true rural doctor of counter-magic can bring out the poison from blood in case of snakebite and other bites of poisonous creatures with the help of *Mantra* and cure the patients.

The Hindu scriptures as well as science believe in the fact that the sound is the primary cause of any creation. The sound is treated as *Brahma* or *Sabda Brahma*, the soul in the Hindu scriptures. Science also proves that it is nothing but the explosion of the sperm and the ovum at the time of mating in the ovary that results in the creation of sound. In other words, the fertilization takes place from that very moment of the creation of sound. This principle is also applicable to the plants though it takes place beyond our observation. This sound creation at the time of fertilization goes with the living being created in the ovary till its death.

According to the Hindu scriptures the five principles of life are Sound (*Sabda*), Sensation (*Sparsha*), Resemblance (*Rupa*), Essence (*Rasa*) and Fragrance (*Gandha*). Out of these five, the sound plays a vital role in the treatment of patients, as with the help of stethoscope in Allopathic and Homoeopathic treatment. Instead of a stethoscope the *Ojhas* conduct *Nadichalana Pariksha* or examination of pulse with the help of *Mantras*. *Bija Mantra*, the vital counter-magic, is applied even in attaining *Brahma* – the *Atman* as established by the scriptures.

Daiba Chikitsa Paddhati

People in eastern India define this method of treatment as *Jaldhaldiya*, a wholesome submission of self to gods for fulfilment of aspirations. In other words, it is known as *Adhiyapada*, lying flat in front of gods or goddesses.

Ishsan is the god worshipped in this form. It is believed that besides curing all diseases this method can also help to achieve god's blessings or godliness. But in the rural areas this measure is usually applied for treatment of diseases.

According to the Hindu scriptures while *Brahma*, the god of creation of all living beings, was in meditation for finding out a measure of creation of creatures, he came across an enlightened and stronger being appearing before him who helped him in the creation. This being is divided into eight parts or factors each representing specified items of creations.

Name		Enlightened	Factor or Image
Rudra	-	Surya	Sun
Bhaba	-	Mahi	Earth
Shiva	-	*Jala*	Water
Pashupati	-	*Banhi*	Fire
Isha	-	*Bayu*	Air
Bhima	-	*Akash*	Sky
Ugra	-	*Dikshita*	
Mahadeva	-	*Chandra*	Moon

According to above description *Isha* is air. But the word can be variously pronounced. When emphasis is given to vowels I and A the pronunciations are *Ishsha* or *Ishaa*. At the same time when emphasis is on nose the pronunciation is *Ishshan* and when inner nose the pronunciation is *Ishsham*. The scriptures say air is life and life is air. So the *Bhagavadgita* says nothing can destroy the soul being *Isha*. *Isha* exists in every living being in the form of *Pranbayu, Apan Bayu, Saran Bayu, Udan Bayu* and *Byan Bayu* being the smallest of the smallest of an object. This fact is also known to the rural *Ajha* and this knowledge forms part of their treatment. The saints have attained this truth. Those, who have attained this truth, they feel no difference among the tenses like the present, the past and the future. Some *Adivasi Ojhas* have also that power.

It is described in the *Purana* that the *Yogis* or the saints attain the Eight Supernatural blessings and they are like *Anima, Lakhima, Mahima, Ishatwa, Kamabashayeta, Prati, Prakashya* and *Vashitwa*. Among these blessings the *Ishatwa* is very significant and effective. A man becomes cursed or blessed by these blessings. We should scientifically investigate to bring out the inner truth that lies in these practices. The Mantras of tribal people, the system of *Ishshan Sadhana*, the *Pothis* (Books) on these practices should be brought to the knowledge of public. This will enable the coming generation to accept and practice an alternative method of treatment.

7

Bengalee–Santal Equation
Dialectics of Identity and Assimilation

Sankar Sengupta

Imagine the sufferings and agony of a community with their independent ethnic identity and unique philosophy of life as they find themselves in the role of a protagonist struggling for their continued existence in a multilingual and multicultural society in accordance with their social institutions and cultural pattern in different states of our democratic country. Their presence in at least 5 states of India and Bangladesh, with the second largest concentration in West Bengal, invites the social scientists to a scenario of a complex process of socio-philosophical transformation of a community in different theatres of culture and power. The present study is about 20 lakh Santals of West Bengal and their Bengali speaking neighbours, certain aspects of their mutual relation and value-oriented response to changing social realities of the contemporary world.

Any discourse on tribal life and culture in this country should begin with the admission of 'little done and the undone vast'. While our anthropologists have done their best to understand the tribal scenario in India, with particular emphasis on the cultural aspect, scholars from other disciplines, specially the social historians have been, to say the least, indifferent to this area of our national life. This gap between the scholar and his subject follows from certain limitations of our life and academics. The first is our legacy of maintaining distance from the marginalized, while in academics even the scholars with more liberal mind-set are not always aware of the singular importance of the cultural perspective and equipped with necessary multidisciplinary tools for a true to life analysis of Indian life–with all its diverse and colourful manifestations. Eminent anthropologists studied the question of identity and assimilation of Indian tribes but social historians failed to analyze the course of interaction among different cultural trends and thus understand the real dimension of the changes affecting our society through the ages.

This brings us to the relevance of the philosophical perspective, to the understanding of philosophy of life of communities, crucial for our comprehension of the Indian reality. Our Institute,[1] in its search for the meaning of lives of people in their own context, accepts the concepts of cultural regions and cultural logic. We accept the rationality and the unique character of the cultural logic for different social groups discernible in the synthetic picture of Indian Civilization through ages. We accept the formulation of Dr. Bernard S. Cohn that in Indian villages different communities have different pasts, all interwoven in the grand design of a civilization.[2]

For the present I would like to confine myself to West Bengal and try to understand the dialectics of identity and assimilation in this complex laboratory of a state. In this state the question of cultural transformation of tribal society cannot be examined in isolation without keeping in mind the historical fact of the pre-eminence of Bengali-speaking people in Bengal and parts of Bihar and Orissa during the colonial period and the resultant social and cultural domination of tribal people by the former, although both were engaged from time to time in a common struggle against the colonial rulers.

For the purpose of our present study we have also to keep in mind that for both Bengalees and Santals the superstructure has had abiding influence on the course of their history. Sometimes grave economic issues become matters of academic interest while the question of rituals and similar issues create noticeable social commotion. The role of the cultural substratum becomes apparent as the Santal resistance often takes the form of rigid adherence to their religious norms to dissociate themselves from the world of the 'Diku', though specific grounds of discontent are more often their marginalization and economic exploitation. For the Bengalee gentleman recent experiences of Gorkhaland

and Kamtapur make him suspicious of the Santal demand for the implementation of Article 29 of the constitution.[3] But his keen sense of culture also makes him appreciative of the richness of Santal way of life and in fact he is even ready to learn certain things from his tribal neighbour notwithstanding his cultural vanity, only if the political world allows the communion.

In the colonial period tribals suffered in the hands of traders, moneylenders and landlords. Marginalization of tribals through land alienation and consequent pauperization continued unabated even after independence. As the State replaced the colonial agent, big public sector projects and large-scale conversion of agricultural land into non-agricultural for urbanization made the bourgeoisie model of development led by the Multi National Companies thoroughly unacceptable to the tribals. While the Bengali-speaking majority assimilated minor tribal groups through Hindu method of absorption abetted by cultural domination, Santals of West Bengal continue to maintain their cultural identity.

In their struggle against cultural inroads the dignified Santals always take recourse to passive resistance. They steadfastly follow their own ritual and seldom disown the community. This adherence to their own belief system is universal. The migrant workers of the Tea gardens of north Bengal, migrant agricultural labourers scattered throughout the state, poor peasants in the mixed villages of Midnapur, Bankura, Purulia and Birbhum, emotionally more stable peasantry near Jharkhand borders–even the small salaried middle class living in the cities–everywhere the Santal community, in varying degrees, share these distinct cultural traits upholding basic values of a happy community life and protecting the integrity of the community. It is true that in recent period certain segments of tribal society show signs of decadence. But by and large the underlying resilience derived from basic integrity of this society is still discernible. Their beliefs and practices–the rites of fertility, rites for the dead, harmonious man–nature, man-woman and adult-child relationship, their ethic and rich cultural heritage of folklore and songs have enriched Indian civilization. Adept agriculturists since ancient times, they have evolved through the centuries a sound system of community life in the villages based on co-operation and interdependence, equality and friendship, love and mutual trust.

The Jharkand movement and the formation of the Jharkand state boosted tribal morale to hold their own against the threat of disintegration of their culture emanating from certain aberrations of Indian politics perpetrated by the Fundamentalists impatiently pursuing their programme of absorption of tribal communities in the so called mainstream. In fact both Bengalees and Santals have survived this menace, thanks mainly to the inherent vitality of their cultural life. But for the Santals their cultural bonds with their ethnic brethren across the border is much more significant historically as the source of their empowerment. Administrative border is no doubt important but more important is the human tie, which gathered strength through centuries of sustained stress and exploitation. Even if we take into consideration multiple identities of the Santals living in West Bengal, the psychological ground they share with their Bengalee neighbour is insignificant compared to the historic cultural bond with their ethnic brethren of Jharkand. Santals are fully conscious of their heritage in their own way. Bengalees and for that matter all Indians ought to share this heritage with their tribal brethren and such realization is essential for uniting our people. In his Presidential address in the Asiatic Society, Calcutta in the year 1999 Prof. Dilip Kumar Biswas pointed out that "the Buddhist text Manjusrimulakalpa gives us the very important information that the people of Vanga, Samatata, Harikela Gauda and Pundra were speakers of the Asura language which happens to be still a surviving specimen of a dialect of the Kol-Munda group. The cumulative evidence of ethnology and linguistics so far summarized perhaps thus leaves us in no doubt that the Austro – Asiatic formed the earliest level of India's language culture on which the subsequent historical civilization of the land rests".

Our first Prime Minister, Jawaharlal Nehru, had this understanding of history and had the good fortune of sharing the wisdom of experts like Verrier Elwin and Prof. Nirmal Kumar Bose. Prof. Bose in his famous lecture before the Indian Science Congress Association in the year 1941 observed "today the problem of establishing democratic society in India has become a pressing one. But although, on the whole, Hindu Society is one yet there are differences among its social classes, which have to be made up before we can combine as a nation unified in political aspiration as well as in national action. It is necessary therefore that a scientific enquiry into the character of Hindu social organization should precede any activity towards the end".

The nation was not unified and the tribal policy of Nehru Government could never be implemented in detail because of socio-economic constraints, which were more real than the pious announcements from the floor of the Parliament. Mr. Bhabani Sen, one of the front-ranking leaders of Bengal, wrote brilliant articles on the tribal situation in the country and upheld the issue of identity of tribals for strengthening the forces of integration. But as usual there were very few takers. The economic compulsion of profit market society and the vanity of the Bengalee gentleman nurtured by a strong cultural movement and the Hindu method of tribal absorption – all combined together to dilute this all-important question of identity of tribal society. Moreover, post-partition Bengalee psyche reacted sharply to any change in the Bengalee–tribal equation. This is the irony of history that in this background came the present ruling elite to shoulder the responsibility of so called modernization of tribes and in some places over enthusiastic political activists were instrumental in creating tension over *Jaher Than* and tribal rituals which alienated the tribals and unleashed chaos in certain areas of West Bengal that ultimately paved the way for anarchy engineered by anti people forces. Somehow Bengalee intellectuals missed the point that 'reformation' can wait, recognition of identity can never.

In such a difficult and tense situation, historians need 'fewer sources and stouter boots' to unveil the mystery of the psyche of the generally secretive and apprehensive tribal population. Archives are artificial artifacts. So a social historian has to move from village to village for acquaintance with the inside view of tribal society and thus get an authentic data of tribal perception of the changes in our plural society and the way the tribals respond to these changes guided by their own value system and their philosophy of life. Recent survey in the countryside reveals certain indications that the community is opening up to suggestions of closer ties with their Bengalee neighbours.

In recent times there is a perception in tribal society of the possibility of a shift in the attitude and the policy of the establishment. It appears that the establishment has become more sensitive to the intricacies of tribal culture and has initiated steps to promote Santali language and literature. And in the countryside they are becoming more tolerant and appreciative of tribal rituals and practices. Urban intellectuals and village folk belonging to the Santal community, who seem to have been impressed by this change, are definitely in a minority. Still this perception deserves careful examination as there is always a probability that the theoreticians in the ruling circle, baffled in their complex task of manipulating power equations in a bourgeoisie society, might go back to their original formulations, which allow more space for Bengalee-Santal amity.

What is more interesting for our study is the orientation of the tribal psyche, which makes them appreciative of such manoeuvers. This vulnerability can be explained if we keep in mind the cultural moorings of the community and the prevailing social tension centering round the question of language and culture. Let the social scientist note that here the issue is not one of economic gain or political advantage but a simple gesture of recognition of a culture, a good neighbourly stance of a gentleman.

This receptive appreciation also reveals the truth that like other marginalized groups, tribals also are not aware of the conspiracy of circumstances governing their life in this country. Many minor tribes have been gradually assimilated and absorbed in the mainstream and this process, I fear, will be accelerated in the coming days under the influence of merry go round liberalization and globalization allowing 'fullest freedom of capitalist intercourse'. If we accept this reported tribal perception of change of mind of powers that be as a social reality in West Bengal, we enter a new era when the minor tribes are fully vanquished, while the Santals enjoy a pride of place with state guarantee of full blossoming of their cultural life and tribal elite share the fruits of power with their Bengalee counterpart. The helplessness and cynicism inherent in the whole situation becomes apparent as we note that there is no Santal proletariat as historically the ruling classes saw to it that an ethnically constituted sub-proletariat or 'proletarian vagabonds' would serve their purpose better. Our well to do Santal peasants, however small in number, keenly await modernization of agriculture while the landless and migrant agricultural labourers of the community have no leadership on whom they can depend. In the cities cultural crisis of the urban middle class is apparent from their faceless existence as conflicting emotional loyalties create a psychological void for these people. While agreeing with Prof. Ramdayal Munda that tribal mind is not working out of nervousness and desperation, we also notice signs of strain and vulnerability of the cultural existence of even the vocal and apparently confident Bengali-speaking majority faced with strong waves of a new acculturation sponsored by the votaries of globalization.

From this perspective there is a distinct possibility of Bengalee-Santal rapprochement in the present situation as both are targets of a cultural offensive unleashed by the agents of capitalism in this unipolar world. The other historical possibility in the opposite direction is the strengthening of centrifugal forces so far as West Bengal is concerned. The geographical area covered by the northern part of Orissa and Jharkand with contiguous tribal habitation of West Bengal might generate a strong ethnic movement based on cultural solidarity of the tribal population in this area. Students of psycho-history know that this movement has also the potentiality of freeing the tribal mind of the present anarchic desperation and thus giving birth to the third possibility of happy cultural fusion in our state, strengthened by the socio-economic forces of change strong enough to usher in new equations of life to uphold the glory that is India.

Thus history has placed these two communities in a situation where the all-important cultural question is for the present the only agenda to pursue. This logic of life is reinforced historically as it is clear from their tradition that the Santals know how to live and this art of living is their culture. No wonder, culturally active Bengalees in their new initiative have already won a section of their neighbours. However, social historians will keep their watch beyond the present pragmatic equation expecting a better tomorrow of cultural fusion in a free democratic polity.

References

Ashin Dasgupta Institute of Tribal History, Calcutta (established 1995), 35/2, Adhar Chandra Das Lane, Kolkata 700067.

Bernard S. Cohn, *An Anthropologist among the Historians and other Essays*, Oxford University Press, Delhi,1990.

According to article 29 of Indian Constitution a cultural or linguistic minority has right to conserve its language or culture. The article provides protection to ST communities to preserve their languages, dialects and cultures. The State would not by law enforce upon it any other culture or language.

8

Socio-Religion of the Tribes of West Bengal

Tapashi Ghosh

This paper seeks to say something about the philosophy of life of the tribals of West Bengal. It is true that we have progressed much in every sphere including social and cultural, but even today there are some societies, which may still be called 'primitive, in comparison to the technologically advanced people residing in different cities. The word 'primitive' as applied to the tribes may be viewed in the sense in which Sir James Frazer uses the term i.e. the most elementary classes, the tribal societies. Gradually when they came under the influence of urban life, their culture was affected much. The primitive culture still survives through the mode of thought, manners and customs.

There are many ways by which we may approach the study of tribal life. One of the ways, which I prefer to discuss here, is from the cultural aspect and that too from a specific point of view, which is religion and art. But I will confine my discussion only to West Bengal. West Bengal is such a state where we find many tribal societies. It is not possible to discuss about all of them. So I have selected a particular area – Midnapur, Birbhum and Bishnupur for this purpose. How culture has shaped their pattern of life, their mode of behaviour, their artistic sense and taste, while keeping their originality intact, will be my main concern.

Rapid improvement is going on in the village areas of West Bengal. As a result the social structure along with rites and rituals and the thinking of people are undergoing changes. But I fear that it will be difficult in future to write any history of this changing culture because of the scarcity of testimonies. That is why thorough research leading to scientific knowledge is of utmost necessity. Hopefully in spite of today's changing societies and culture we notice an indomitable eagerness among the researchers to know the value of our own culture and its positive aspects.

Before the spread and establishment of Aryan culture there was a vast heritage of non-Aryan culture in West Bengal, the horizon of which dates back to Paleolithic Age. The weapons of the various stages of the Stone Age have been discovered within the geographical limits of West Bengal. From Chotanagpur and Santal Parganas to the northern highland of the West Bengal the cultural supremacy of the Proto–Austroloid or Nisadas was a historical fact. Hunting, livestock farming, agriculture etc. were the different strata of culture. These different strata were directly linked with the natural environment. In order to know a culture one must know the livelihood of the people of that place. The tradition of hunting and life-stock farming is still alive among some tribes. If we take the instance of Santals in West Bengal we find that though they are now living on agriculture, they have not left the habit of hunting. Moreover, we find the importance of livestock farmers in tribal life. Gopebhum areas in Burdwan district may be cited as an instance.

In the opinion of an old royal descendent if a bear dies they have to observe taboo or '*Asaucha*'. This shows that bear was one of the main animals among all others, which they tame, and the bear was the totem of a branch or clan of the farmers. This is the evidence that they have not left their natural habit of livestock farming. So the long cultural heritage of the people of West Bengal, belonging from different food procuring groups, cannot be denied.

Religion is generally associated with rites and rituals. These rites and rituals are always condition-based, mostly based on geographical conditions. The landforms, the natural vegetation, the minerals, the agricultural products and the forest resources are all related with rites and rituals and hence with religion. That is why we find the observation of taboo even after the death of a bear because to the people of that place bear is not only an animal of reverence but it is quite beneficial and found in large numbers.

A special aspect of culture is the religion proper. Once there was a system of worshiping of Dharma Pillars among some branches of Nisada community. In the pre-Ashoka era also there was such a system of creation of stone pillars with image of animals in the crown. In the primitive age we find totem pillars, which were the objects of reverence. In the later days *Gadura dhawaja* of Vishnu, *Makara dhawaja* and *Vṛṣa dhawaja* of Shiva are said to be its expression. The cult of pillars crowned by such figures was evidently an element of the primitive religion of eastern India. The pre-historic non-Aryan pillar worship, tree and animal worship were practised in Buddha era. In course of time the megalithic culture of stone pillar worship transformed itself into non-Aryan symbol worship of Shiva or Rudra devata. The non-Aryan linga worship of Shiva became Aryanized in later days.

A noteworthy ceremony of Jhargram is the ceremony of *Indra Dhawaja.* A mythological story is behind it. The story runs thus – being defeated in the battle with Asura, Devaraja Indra took refuge with Brahma and Vishnu. Vishnu was pleased and he presented him a garlanded umbrella, which we call *malyachatra* with bells in it and a divine flag, which we call *divyadhawaja.* Indra won the battle against the Asura with that *dhawaja* or flag. Then Indra offered that flag to Chedipati. Chedipati performed all rites and rituals when worshiping it, and on being pleased with him Devaraja Indra ordered 'The King who will worship the flag in this way will have plenty of wealth and grains and he will succeed in all works'. It appears that this *puja* was started from the Vedic era. When the Aryans defeated the non-Aryans in battles and became rulers, from then they started celebrating their victory in this way.

However, mythological stories indicate the fact that the Aryans could not easily defeat the non-Aryans everywhere. Many of the non-Aryans used to live in jungles and worship big trees also. Did the Aryans transform this tree worshiping of non-Aryans to *dhawaja* ceremony through royal functions? Indra is the king of all *Devatas* and umbrella is the royal symbol. That is why sal tree is decorated in this way to make *Indra Dhawaja* and the royal symbol thus turns into a royal ceremony. Thus the name of the ceremony is also *Indra Dhawaja.*

The main reason for performance of this ceremony at Manbhum, Bankura, Midnapur is that the history of these areas is almost the same. The story of capturing the throne and becoming a king is a common thing found in the Santal dominated areas, which runs very well with the mythological story of Devas and Asuras. When different dynasties established their kingdom then the ceremony of *Indra Dhawaja* was established in the shape of victory ceremony. What we actually find here in the celebration of *Indra Dhawaja* on the western border of West Bengal is that the sal tree which is decorated in the fashion of an umbrella is not only depicting the history of collision between the Aryans and non-Aryans, details of which are missing from the pages of ancient history, but also giving the hints of influence of geography, the natural vegetation on the evolution of folk culture. The region where we find this *dhawaja* worship is mainly dominated by sal trees. These sal trees became the symbol to which all rites and rituals are centered. So symbolism plays a great role here and symbolism itself is the mark of high mental level. We also find later-Vedic religion giving much stress on symbolization.

Symbol worship is a special feature in the culture of northeast India. In many places of Rarh, this worship is still in vogue. We find many symbols, which form not only a part of ritual but is also worshiped and revered in Vedic religion. It appears that Kurma symbol is a sign of Kurma totem of one of the Nisada community. Before explaining 'Kurma' as the mythological *Avatara* of Vishnu or the incarnation of Vishnu, it is necessary to think what is the origin of the imagination of *Avatara*? [Matsya, Kurma, Baraha etc.] Why it became necessary for the author of mythology to imagine this *Avatara*? Was it not because of preaching religion among the vast mass of people living at Rarh who were the holder and carrier of totem culture? The ancestral title or the *kaulika upadhi* like 'Bagh', 'Hanti', 'Ghora', etc. of West Bengal is a proof for this. All these tribes were under the influence of Buddhism and Jainism, later of Hinduism also. The combination and unification of these religious practices and culture seem to have transformed the religious god or *dharma thakura* to village deity or *gram devata* at Rarh. His birth ceremony is being observed as '*Gajan*' here.

Gradually the Brahmin priests transformed this '*Gajan*' into a ceremony for the worship of Shiva. Shiva gradually became village deity and ultimately *Gajan* of religion was transformed into *Gajan* of Shiva.

Now, if we turn our attention to the field of art, that art which is related to religion, then we find there also a great philosophical significance. From Santal dominated areas of Jhargram to Bishnupur and Arambagh the images of elephant, horses, made up of burnt clay, are made by local potters in those places where we found village deities. I have seen myself the use of these images at the time of the worship of the village deities. They use this clay image when they promise to offer a particular sacrifice to a deity on fulfilment of a prayer. If the patterns of the images of these elephants, horses are examined thoroughly it will be seen that this clay modelling is progressing towards an imaginative formation deviating gradually from the realistic pattern. The pattern of the images of elephants and horses made in the developed villages of Jhargram has assumed a new look.

One may ask is the natural inclination in the development of style of arts from realism to symbolism? Or nature comes first, then symbol? Or to be more precise reality first, symbol signifying artistic independence later? It may also be that both have developed simultaneously. Many people think the trend of development of the manner of art is from practicality or reality to symbolization, from representational depiction to conventionalized manner and style. Even in the eyes of a tribal artist some particular part of a perceived object becomes so imaginary that giving a shape to that particular part seems to be true or real to him. From that the symbolic art developed. This is also true in the case of elephants, horses made of clay in West Bengal. It is interesting to note that clay modelling of Krishnanagar is mainly representational but of realistic nature. Therefore, we find different pattern and style in different areas. The pattern and style of arts have not developed mechanically based on fixed and chalked out design. Due to difference in regional social and mental make up, they tend to exhibit varieties.

Due to the collision between different cultures the regional culture changes its shape and through actions and interactions new integrations are formed. Clash and contact come from two different sides. It may be traced as Aryan – non-Aryan, Hindu-Buddhist, Shakta-Baishnab etc. It may be regarded as a conflict of cultural trend form within. The depth of assimilation in every stratum of culture is not however the same. It is mainly dependable on the receptive power and propensity of people of different strata.

So long we are not familiar with the diversity of culture it is not possible to establish a deep-rooted unity. Greater unity may be formed with the union of small diversities and independence. The unity of Indian culture is based on diversity of culture of many castes and tribes.To judge this diversity it is necessary to have regional level research and study. But here I want to draw attention to such questions as – are the arts, paintings and crafts the products of uncivilized mind or they are the product of highly imaginative thinking? The clay models of horse and elephant show that they are not the true copies of the original. Is it that due to their uncivilized nature tribal artists do not know the art of exact copying or they are so much imaginative that they are rejecting reality and are running towards abstraction? Again is their thinking influenced by Hindu myth and Vedic civilization? I propose that they had not copied every thing exactly, but modified them in their own light. Though the different cultures have influenced the life style of present day tribal society, still in spite of regional differences we find their primitive nature often exhibited in their artistic creations and this primitive nature is more or less the same through out India. This may be the reason why we notice basic similarity in the art of different tribal societies the underlying philosophy of which is the amalgam of reality. As I say this I have in mind the cave painting at Bhimbaithka in Madhya Pradesh and the clay model of the animals of the Santal society, which I have referred earlier.

Acknowledgements

I am grateful to Indian Council of Philosophical Research, Lucknow for their kind help and financial aid without which it would not have been possible for me to pursue my work.

References

Benedict, Ruth, *Patterns of Culture,* Pelican Books, 1946.

Chandra, R.P., *The Beginnings of the Art in Eastern India,* An.S.I., Memoir No. 30.

Chandra, R.P., 'Survival of the Prehistoric Civilization of the Indus Valley', Anthropological Survey of India, Memoir No. 41, Human Sacrifice.

Kroeber, A.L., Anthropology, London, Revised Edition, 1948.

Majumdar, R. C., (ed.), *History of Bengal,* Vol. II, Dacca, 1943.

Malinowski, B., *The Dynamics of Cultural Change,* Yale University Press, London, 1945.

Sarkar, Dinendra, 'Spread of Aryanism in Bengal', *Journal of the Asiatic Society of Bengal,* Vol:18, No. 2, 1952.

Zenaide, A. Ragozin, *Vedic India,* Oriental Book Sellers and Publishers, Delhi, 1961.

9

Forest People, Modern People
Modernity and Social Change among the Ho and Munda People of Jharkhand

Barbara Verardo

In the relevant Indian literature, Sanskritization and Westernization constitute two related yet different phenomena. First introduced by Srinivas,[1] the term Sankritization refers to the process by which low caste Hindus imitate and adopt the moral values and codes of behaviour of high-caste Hindus to raise their social status. Thus, 'Sanskritization can be seen not only as an idiom of mobility but also as an important source of *continuity with the past.* Its symbols and values are essentially those of the traditional order.[2] By contrast, when 'the modern secular social order provides *alternative symbols and values* which are likely to become increasingly important in the future', we can talk of Westernization.[3]

In the same line, Dumont had noted how low-caste Hindus tend to *sanskritize* where upper-caste ones *westernize* instead: 'caste values envelop and encompass modern ferments. One could find no better demonstration... of how powerless are modern education and social and political transformation *to overthrow the traditional system'*[4] (emphasis mine).

Westernization and modernization are often used as synonymous in the Indian literature. And both are generally put in opposition to Sanskritization: 'At a time when a *modernist* élite is trying to push the country towards a secular and *Westernized* social order, ... those who had in the past occupied a fairly low social position may set themselves up as the bastions of social values [i.e. they Sanskritize]'[5] (emphasis mine).

The present paper gives ethnographic evidence of a specular case. By adopting the perspective of the people under study, the present paper deals with a case in which people, by imitating and adopting moral values and codes of behaviour of high-caste Hindus, not only *sanskritize* but also *modernize*.

The paper deals with the Munda and Ho people of a forested village in Porahat area, in the district of West Singhbhum in Jharkhand in central India. Hos and Mundas are classified as Scheduled Tribes by the Indian Constitution, and share a common language, territory and cultural traits with only slight differences. The purpose of this paper is to show how, from the perspective of the people under study, adoption of 'caste values' does indeed correspond to an 'overthrow of the traditional [tribal] system'. To be able to claim a higher status, people must reject their own past, both symbolically and practically. And they find in caste values a new, *modern*, continuity and source of legitimacy.

As Deliege remarked about the Bhils of Western India:[6] 'When a tribal section becomes more Hinduised, it ... becomes ashamed of its [habits and customs] and tries to deny or conceal them. This sense of inferiority ... is perhaps the best indicator of a transformation of a tribal group into a caste since it denotes a loss of its dignity, its pride, its sense of equality and its independence'. In the case under study, higher-status claims are encouraged and legitimised by conversion to a *Bhagat* movement locally defined as *Shiuli dharom.*[7] *Bhagat* movements constitute a common means for Sanskritization and represent a widespread phenomenon in India among low-caste Hindus and tribal people. They are devotional movements which normally require their followers to subscribe to upper-caste practices and to completely reject 'tribal' or low-caste norms and rituals.

Although both Hos and Mundas can convert and become followers, it is however a fact that the *Shiuli dharom* has historically been associated mainly with the Mundas.[8] Through conversion, Mundas attempt to 'liberate' themselves from their 'shameful' past, at least ideologically if not in practice. Notwithstanding the obvious continuity in daily practices, Mundas publicly and explicitly reject their 'habits and customs'. At the same time, they adopt and imitate high-caste Hindus' values and practices, perceived as vehicles for 'civilisation' and modernity.

Conversion to the *dharom* leads to the crystallization of caste boundaries between Hos and Mundas, who used to be 'of the same kind', and the development of a new 'kind' of people among the converts. By claiming a higher social status vis-à-vis the Hos and the non-converts, the Mundas are transforming flexible social and cultural distinctions into rigid and clear-cut boundaries, with both intermarriages and commensality being strictly prohibited. The distinction has a political counterpart, too.[9] Hos support the Jharkhand ('Land of forest') political party, which has been fighting for tribal autonomy from the Bihar state since the end of the nineteenth century,[10] whilst Mundas sympathise with the Bharatiya Janata Party (BJP), the ruling party.[11] As we shall see, this divergence in political preferences reflects opposed sources of legitimacy: on the one hand, the forest, its spirits, and the ancestors, on the other, the State and the 'modern' world.

A Social Forgetting of the Past

Since the very first days of my eighteen-month fieldwork in a forested village of Jharkhand, *Shiuli*[12] converts kept on emphasising their differences vis-à-vis the non-converts: could not I see how *modern* and *civilized* they were, compared to the others? I remember paying almost no attention to those statements. I was looking for 'the real stuff' and 'exotic curiosities', and not for people claiming to be westernized! However, I was soon to realise how ethnocentric my assumption was. The model for modernity was not given by the Western world, but by moral values and codes of behaviour of high-caste Hindus and by the life-style of the cities.

The main change brought about by conversion to *dharom* consists in the replacement of affines with Hindu specialists to perform rites of passage. According to the Mundas, only Hindu specialists can 'clean' (*sappa*) dirt away. It is however my suggestion that what they really wipe away from their bodies, houses and landscape, are not just ritual impurities but what they referred to as 'the rule from the past', 'the path of the ancestors', or again as the 'words of the old ones'.

Conversion also implies a radical change in religious beliefs and practices. *Bhagat* movements generally act as powerful vehicles for disseminating modern reformist hostility to animal sacrifice and the *Shiuli dharom* constitutes no exception. From their onset, the traditional faith generally declines and new gods and beliefs are introduced: 'A Bhagat is basically one who has consciously renounced faith in the primitive cult, labelled animistic, and developed faith in Hindu gods and the associated religious principles. Further, he is one who has given up many old practices and taken to new ones which are considered essential requirements of the new faith'.[13]

Converts have abandoned the ritual offering of animals by adopting vegetarian deities. Carnivorous spirits are stripped off of their benevolent nature and are dreadfully feared. People would carefully avoid even talking about them. In other words, their existence is acknowledged, but they are neither appeased nor dealt with. Similarly, collective festivals are rejected, with old and young generations of converts not joining their dances and songs and observing them from a distance only.

The giving up of alcohol drinking represents a similarly explicit step towards Sanskritization. Rice-beer plays a fundamental role both in religious practices and social domain too. The preparing and the sharing of rice-beer *de facto* creates 'relatedness'. Not only rice-beer is indicated as a marker of tribal identity, but the mythological and primordial incest between siblings, which gave rise to humankind, was also beleived to have been both caused and excused by rice-beer intoxication.[14] By rejecting its use, people not only create distinctiveness, but further crystallize the boundary between past and present.

The main break with tradition is however represented by the rejection of ancestors' worship and clan graveyards. *Converts* have also abandoned the 'Calling of the soul' ceremony, which ritually connects the kitchen, abode of the soul of ancestors, with the clan cemetery. Both kitchen and graveyards produce and negotiate clan memberships, being symbolic spaces for social reproduction and continuity between the dead and the living.

Converts have substituted the ceremony with different practices performed by Hindu specialists. When they die, they become malevolent spirits rather than benevolent ancestors. Instead of being ritually *called back* in their houses, the 'old and sleeping ones', as they are also called, undergo a collective process of 'social forgetting', and my simple mentioning of them was often a cause of embarrassment–and seen as source of danger. Old kitchens need periodical and weekly blessings and in some cases they are destroyed altogether at the time of the household's conversion and substituted by new ones.

Similarly, most converts fear clan graveyards and would avoid crossing them especially after dark. This attitude clearly contrasts with that of non-converts, who would instead conduct many social activities precisely within graveyards' boundaries. More importantly, converts have stopped burying their dead in their clan graveyards. These have been substituted by individual tombs made of cement and placed in households' gardens instead. People see them as a sign of 'modernity' and as something that 'people of the town' have.

To them, what really matters is not the sharing of a common burial ground after death, but that of a common place of worship during life. The sharing of different sacred spaces produces different social memberships and religious affiliations replace clan ties. It is not graveyards but *Shiuli* temples that reflect or negotiate people's social affiliations. It is not the past, i.e. ancestors and their bones, that legitimizes the present, but the present that legitimizes itself through a new set of rules, codes of behaviours and a new sacred landscape.

The rejection of clan graveyards as sacred spaces is accompanied by a parallel denial of them as legal evidence of land possession. The more old a graveyard is, the more the presence of a clan in the territory is locally legitimized. The sacred link between people and land starts with the transformation of virgin tracts of forest into cultivable land, in the subsequent preparation of the soil for cultivation, in the growing and harvesting of paddy, in the nurturing of one household's members with it, and ends with the burying of human remains in the clan's land and the calling back of their souls into the house. Clan graveyards then stand as icons of the sacred relationship between people and land. The same relationship has a political dimension, too, as clan graveyards are conceptualized as legal evidence of territorial belonging and land rights. People would constantly refer to their past to legitimize their present, hence our need to look at history to understand the 'here and now'.

The nineteenth century was characterized by tribal revolts against land dispossession caused by the colonial codification[15] which transformed rajas into landlords and symbolic contributions into payments of rent. The Porahat area in particular was the centre of some of the major tribal revolts in Chotanagpur such as the great Kol rebellion of 1832, the Sardar *Andolan* and the Birsa *Andolan* of 1895-1900. In the village under study, '*the money was never paid ... and from 1830 to 1836 the whole body of aboriginals resisted all attempts to realise rent, and waged war on the claimants ... because of the attempt of the tenure-holder to destroy* [land] *rights amongst them, through the imposition of the plough tax and the introduction of diku* [non-tribal] *headmen*'.[16]

What people were resisting to was not only the payment of rent but the policy of the Forest department. From the 1840s onwards the East India Company attempted to exercise a monopoly right of timber extraction from the forests. At the end of the century, forest reserves were established under the control of the Forest department. Shifting cultivation was seen as a destructive practice, forest officials sought to encourage sedentarism.

People used clan graveyards as title deeds, i.e. as evidence of their belonging to those lands, hence of those lands belonging to them. The British eventually understood the indigenous concept and used it as criterion for their records of rights. The presence of clan graveyards became sufficient proof of 'prior ownership of the jungle' during the settlement and record-of-rights operations of 1903-7.[17]

In this way, the spiritual and ritual connection between land and people acquired *de jure* meanings with the British. The indigenous notion was accorded legal status and was considered as sufficient evidence for everlasting legal rights on all land cleared and prepared by them or their ancestors, unless they had sold their interest, and for colonising rights as well as a privileged fiscal status.

Although the British recognised indigenous customs concerning land and forest, and went as far as to codify them in the Chotanagpur Tenancy Act of 1908, they eventually gave priority to forest conservation and commercialization.[18] In 1895 they classified all forests of Singhbhum into Village, Reserved and Protected Forests, and forcibly evacuated many villages that 'happened' to lie within the last two.[19] The reservation of forests and the consequent forceful eviction of pioneers from their villages was the immediate reason for the insurgence of the Birsa *Andolan* in the Porahat area.

Besides dispossessing the people of their land, the British eventually replaced graveyards with land records as the only legally recognised and valid proof of land ownership. Although land records were initially compiled according to the 'graveyard proof', written papers were meant by the British bureaucracy to replace the ancestral source of legitimacy as title deeds. After the 1907 settlement, in fact, they purposely denied land rights even to those who passed the 'graveyard proof' in order to make the new kind of legitimacy effective.[20]

After Independence, the Bihar government resumed the British policy of forest management. Moreover, in the name of environmental conservation, it imposed state monopolies and new restrictions in the use of forest products. Irrespective of the fact that the livelihood of local people depended almost entirely on forest products, the Bihar government gave big portions of Reserved and Protected Forest of Porahat on lease to a private corporation at the beginning of the 1960s. The 'Corporation' had exclusive rights on the cutting, collection and selling of wood and other forest products. Not only local people had no access to forest resources, but they also received no share from the sale.

As people recall, the Corporation soon eradicated all sal (sacred) trees (Shorea Robusta) as well as other trees and plants essential for the survival of tribals. The Singhbhum forest used to be known as one of the biggest sal tree forest of the world. Today it has almost completely disappeared, because of the state and tribals' exploitation. Once sal trees were eradicated, teak trees were planted in their place, because of their high commercial price and their fast growth. Yet, they do not allow the underwood to grow; so that leaves, roots and mushrooms almost disappeared from tribal diet, and wild animals migrated. People would recall those times by saying that they had nothing to eat, because the 'forest was finishing' (*buru chabakerae:).*

Local men and women were employed to cut, transplant and collect timber. Half of these labourers' salaries were paid with money and half in wheat. Because forest products were not available anymore, and people worked for the Corporation, paddy fields were progressively abandoned. Thus, tribals' survival relied almost exclusively on the Corporation's wheat.

In 1978 they eventually rose into open revolt against the Corporation and local government officials, when the wheat, that labourers received as monthly payment, was found to be spoiled and rotten, hence inedible. People reacted violently by demolishing Forest bungalows and attacking forest guards, contractors and local authorities. That was the beginning of the so-called *Jangol andolan*, or 'Jungle uprising', which eventually extended to all other forested areas of Singhbhum district.

The conflict between state and tribals reached its peak in the middle of the 1980s. Police forces drove people away from their re-settlements. People of the village under study would proudly recall the way they faced the army with bows and arrows adding that they would do the same nowadays, was the Jharkhand party to fail in claiming their land back from the government.

Today rights on land and forest still represent the main cause of tension between tribal people and the State and graveyards are still used as title-deeds against government's claims. Their modes of resistance consist in tree-cutting activities and illegal occupation of old and newly-cleared settlements. Old graveyards identify ancient villages covered by jungle and people would resettle them. By doing so, they assert their colonizing rights and the authority of the ancestors.

Today non-converts are still fighting against the State (*sarkar*). Be it Indian or British, the State has historically been considered an enemy, belonging to the 'outside' world, or '*diku disum*' (*diku*: outsider: *disum*: territory). People who do not live in the forest, do not cut trees and do not have graveyards are usually defined as *diku*. They are conceptualized as people who live in big cities, are educated, wear spectacles and speak Hindi. City-dwellers and government officials are all commonly identified as such. They are described as untruthful, cunning and cheating people.

At the same time, however, *dikus* embody modernity. Modernity is mainly talked about in terms related to cooking and eating habits: both British officials and people of the city are said to use forks and knives rather than hands for eating; they are said to eat white rice and not brown one; to cook with oil and chillies; to look for the 'quality' of their food and not for the 'quantity' of it, and so on.

Converts conceptualize the forest and its dwellers as being at the periphery and margins of society. So they are shifting their loyalty to the State. They have replaced graveyards with land records as proof of land possession. They reject tree-cutting activities and have abandoned the tribal fight against the State. As they say, the forest is an 'Indian national property', and tree cutting activities are not something to be proud of.

Ultimately, *converts* perceive the way people relate to the forest as a source of caste connotations. In the area under study, different kinds of landscape connote different kinds of people, with environmental boundaries corresponding to cultural ones, with small differences in language, pronunciation and customs. Hence, the *Bir-hoko* are those people (*hoko*) who live in the deep forest (*bir*), and perform hunting-and gathering activities; *Buru-hoko* are those who live in the secondary forest (*buru*), and practise slush-and-burn cultivation; and *Hoko* are those who live in permanent villages and practice settled cultivation.

Converts envisage the continuum in evolutionary terms, with 'civilisation' being equated to the 'outside' world, and 'wilderness' equated to 'backwardness'. The Mundas place themselves at the top of this hierarchy, i.e. at the far end of the continuum, while the *Bir-hoko* are the most stigmatised. *Converts* would admit that once upon a time their ancestors were in fact *bir-hoko* and that they must have been the 'same kind' of people as they speak the same language and have identical clan names. While talking about it, they would show some shame but also be proud for the way they managed to 'progress' vis-à-vis the others, who have remained 'half naked, simple-minded and even fool, with poor cooking habits and uneducated'.

Again I believe that both historical reconstruction and the historical imagination can shed interesting insights in the issue. British officials would invariably be talked about as the ultimate representation of 'civilization'. They would be remembered as wearing trousers and eating with forks and knives, a sign, as they would say, of 'modernity'. In addition, their immense power would also be highlighted: tribals carrying colonial officials on their own shoulders for miles and miles, and the threat of extremely painful physical punishments or imprisonment constitute unanimous recollections of the British time.

In colonial understandings, tribes were not barbaric but savage, i.e. they were considered as outside of, or better, before civilization. Hence the colonial paternalistic tones and the identification of tribal people as honest, naive and genuine. As the colonisers had the mastery and conservation of the forest as one of their 'civilising' missions, this was to be obtained through the separation of tribes from forests.

With Independence, the unity of the nation was emphasized and 'tribals' or 'jungli people' became for some to be a source of shame, to be 'civilised' as soon as possible. The *converts* today appear to hold the same notion. Whereas some villagers organised an armed resistance to such transformation, as we saw above, others have instead bought the 'new' ideology. These are those who eventually adopted the *dharom* and who replaced local forest gods with a superior, vegetarian and masculine one, Buddha, a god of the city, who does not belong to the forest.[21]

The detachment of converts from local spirits and ideologies probably contributed to their absorption of the colonial 'enchantments'. Local modes of production became associated with backwardness and the forest acquired a prevalent negative dimension. Indeed, it is only among the converts that we find heads of village, who acted as mediators with the colonial administration, and civil servants (forest guards and teachers). This allowed for an additional source of income independent from seasonal variability and a means for money-lending activities.[22]

Still today, the clearing of forest and the making of new fields are not primary issues for *Converts,* at least for some of them. They have permanent or seasonal stalls in the local market place and have been able to secure an additional source of income and do not depend on harvesting alone. Moreover, *converts,* and only *converts,* have government jobs, either as teachers or forest guards. The making of new fields for the new generation is not envisaged, and other kinds of investments are privileged instead.

Converts are the best educated, some of them having lived for years in town hostels. Even at a later stage in their life, they are those who go to town quite often, even if only for getting their pensions. They own radios and bicycles. They move outside the village more often and easily, hence they do 'know' and imitate the life-style of town people. Some young *converts* told me they will sell their fathers' properties after their death to go and live in the cities. They are, in a sense, the most lured by life in the cities, and the most ashamed by their being or having once been *buru-hoko.*

By detaching themselves from the forest both as a mode of subsistence, as an identity marker and as a spiritual source, it is my suggestion that the *converts* developed a different worldview from the one based on the above-described 'ideology of graveyards' (which revolves around the relation between land and local spirits and which ultimately represents a claim for recognition of primordial pioneering rights). Still today, what they strive for is not the transformation of forest into new cultivable fields, but jobs in the public service, a higher status among their tribal and non-tribal colleagues, and their not being depicted as forest people anymore. Or a passage from forest pride to forest shame.

Ultimately, the 'new' criteria for social status are linked the 'new' concept of wilderness: disassociated from power, the 'land of the forest' is identified instead with marginality, ignorance, backwardness and subordination, whereas 'the land of the plains' is equated with 'civilisation', a space for modernity, sophistication and progress.

To the *converts,* to be 'modern' means to socially and ritually differentiate themselves from the 'forest people'. By sanskritizing, i.e. by adhering to values and behaviours of high-caste Hindus, they become more and more similar to the *dikus*, or a different kind of people. Ultimately, criteria for social status are linked to concepts of *civilization* vs. *wilderness*: disassociated from power, the 'land of the forest' is identified instead with marginality, ignorance, backwardness and subordination. By contrast, 'the land of the plains' is equated with 'civilisation', a space for sophistication, progress and ultimately, modernity.

Notes and References

1. M.N. Srinivas, *Social Change in Modern India,* Berkeley/Los Angeles, University of California Press, 1966.
2. A. Béteille, 'Society and Politics in India', London School of Economics, *Monographs on Social Anthropology* No. 63, Delhi, 1997, p.165.
3. *Ibid.*, p.162.
4. L. Dumont, *Homo Hierarchicus: The Caste System and its Implications*, Chicago: University of Chicago Press, 1980, p. 224.
5. Béteille, Society and Politics, p. 165.
6. R. Deliege, *The Bhils of Western India* : Some Empirical and Theoretical Issues in Anthropology in India, National, Delhi, 1985, p. 160.
7. The *Shiuli dharom* entered the village in the 1930s. *Shiuli* is the name of the village, where it originated, in Gaya district, Bihar. *Dharom* means cosmic or moral order, religion in Hindi.
8. The reasons for such association of Mundas with the *dharom* are quite complex and constitute the subject of a different paper. Moreover, they have no relevance for the purpose of the present paper.
9. Although in practice, social, religious and political distinctions are not so clear-cut, it is however my belief that some general trends do in fact exist.
10. The Jharkhand party represents the 'modern' development of the Birsa Munda millennial movement, which developed in 1895 in the area under study, the Singhbhum district of South Bihar, as a revolt against land and forest dispossession.
11. Apparently in contrast to its nationalist ideology, the BJP fostered the idea of a separate state, in order to penetrate the tribal vote bank. This is called *Vananchal* ('Land of forest', in Hindi)

geographically similar but politically and ideologically opposed to the *Jharkhand*. Eventually, the Jharkhand/Vananchal state was carved out of South Bihar on 15 November 2000.

12. The term *Converts* refers to those members of the Munda and Ho caste who converted to the *Shiuli dharom*. Because the majority of the households who converted belong to the Munda caste, the term generally–but not always-identifies Munda people. Moreover, as we shall see, religious affiliation to the *dharom* is invested with caste connotations, so that Ho converts are *de facto* Mundas, and Munda non-converts are perceived as *transforming* into Hos.

13. K.S. Singh, *Tribal Movements in India,* Vol. 2, New Delhi, Manohar Publications, 1983, p. 313.

14. Rice-beer pertains to the feminine domain. Women only know how to prepare it and which roots to use from the forest. By rejecting its use, *converts* are *de facto* threatening feminine power. It is not a coincidence that women play a key role in the movement of resistance against conversion.

15. In particular the Bengal Permanent Settlement of 1793.

16. T.S. McPherson, Final Report on the Operations for the Preparation of a record of rights in Pargana Porahat, district Singhbhum 1905-1907, Calcutta, 1908, p.18.

17. Porahat Settlement 1906-7, Settlement officers' notes on khuntkatti rights in Porahat Estate, File n.1. E. Lister, Settlement Officer, To: Commissioner of CN, 9.12.05: *'The tendency seems to be to take the existence of a graveyard, once it has been ascertained to cover the corpse of the ancestor of the man who claims it and has not been shown to have been forcibly or fraudulently set up, as practically conclusive proof'*.

18. The Forest Department-Correspondence files in the District Record Room of Chaibasa, headquarters of West Singhbhum district, testify the British officials' conservationist and environmental concerns. At the same time, however, they also document the fact that the forest was primarily a source of timber for railways' construction of and for commercial purposes.

19. See for instance the following extract from hand-written field-notes of Settlement Officers during the Operation of 1903-07: 'There is now very little jungle (comparatively speaking) to be brought under cultivation. What there is has practically been taken for 'protected forests', and it is probably best for all that what has been left out should be preserved as long as possible – which will not be long in any case ... 'The one great encroachment in their rights, (and although it by no means affected all of them it created a general

feeling of dissatisfaction and of distrust of Government which it will take long to line down) was the constitution of the reserved forests in the course of which the tenants were evicted from a considerable number of villages, thereby of course ... their khuntkatti status, for which the grant of raiyati lands elsewhere can never compensate them. Several have asked me whether they would not be able to go back and it is the fear that they will eventually be excluded from the protected forests as they are from the reserved forest that has been at the bottom of most of the opposition to the demarcation'.

20. See for instance the following extract from the above-mentioned hand-written note: 'Even at the risk of interference with ancient custom I think that a rule should be made that no one on whom a right to erect a graveyard is confirmed in future shall in this district be recognised as mundari, whether by adoption into the village family or by the grant by a village family of a ... lean of uncultivated land. Such a course may have been very recently in days gone by where the clearing has been done, but I think that in the future the abuses are likely to outweigh the advantages'.

21. Similar religious crisis following British-induced transformations have been observed among other tribal populations of northern India.

22. Needless to say, rice cultivation remained their primary source of income.

10

Changing Tribal Life of Chotanagpur

Christianity as a Catalyst

Chittaranjan Kumar Paty

Chotanagpur in the present Jharkhand state has been known as the abode of the various tribes such as Mundas, Oraons, Santals, Hos, Kharias and others. They presently constitute about 27% of the total population of Jharkhand state. These tribals had been influenced mainly by Hinduism and Christianity. This paper seeks to study the influence of Christianity as bringing about changes in tribal life.

Christianity came to this region with the coming of British rule. First it was to serve religious needs of the military personnel. As there were some military cantonments at Ramgarh, Hazaribagh and Doranda in Ranchi some European Chaplains were posted in this area. The first Church was built at Hazaribagh in 1842.[1] This marked the beginning of the entry of Christian ideas in indigenous life. But actual proselytization among civil population began when four German Pastors named Emile Schatz, August Brandt, Frederick Batsch and Theodore Janke, arrived in Chotanagpur in 1845. They were sent by Pastor Gossner of Berlin. Actually they were going to Burma but in the meantime they met some tribals of Chotanagpur in the streets of Calcutta. The knowledge of their pitiable condition influenced them and so they decided to move to Chotanagpur. They finally arrived at Ranchi on 2 November 1845. They founded a mission centre on 1 December 1845 at a locality which they named as Bethseda, meaning the House of Piety.[2] This place is presently known as Bethseda Compound of G.E.L. Church, Ranchi. Later on other such missionary groups as Society for the Gospel

(S.P.G.) Mission, Roman Catholic Mission and Christian Missionary Society (C.M.S.) Mission entered this region. All these missionaries started their works since that time. Thus the chanced meeting of some tribals with the missionaries at Calcutta and the coming of the missionaries in Chotanagpur heralded a new phase in the history of Chotanagpur which influenced both tribal and non-tribal life.

The first change was the introduction of an exotic religion and belief system. The missionaries soon set up many Churches in the whole of the region. The Church at Hazaribagh mentioned earlier closed down after the revolt of 1857-58. Meanwhile another Church was founded at Ranchi on 18 November 1851 which was consecrated on the Christmas of 1855. This Church is known as St. Christ Church.[3] Later on several other Churches of different denominations came into existence. Their main centres of activity were Ranchi, Chaibasa, Hazaribagh, Gobindpur, Lohardaga, Murhu, Itki, Sarwada, Maranghada, Ramtolia and other places of this region.[4]

The combined proselytizing activity of Churches succeeded in winning over several tribals into their fold. The converts were mainly from the Munda and Oraon tribes.[5] The number of converts was 11,000 in 1869 which rose to 36,281 in 1881 and again to 6,00,000 in 1967.[6] But among the converts we notice a differential tribe wise representation. According to the census of 1981 the rate of conversion among the tribe was: Mundas 27.7%, Oraons 26%, Santals 3.3% and Hos 1.3%.[7]

The tribals were also influenced by the Christian religious values. There was an inner process of transformation of mind at the imaginative and reflective levels of tribal thought and feelings. The sacrament of Baptism, confirmation of the adult Christian member as a full member of fellowship, solemnization of marriages according to Christian rites and burial of the dead with a strong faith in resurrection at the second coming of Christ gave a new turn of life to the tribal people. The promotion of tribal, Indian and western music in Church had enriched the tribal culture and social life. Besides *Mandar, Nagara* they used western music such as violin, guitar, harmonium and organs also.[8] Now the tribal converts constituted a regular member of the choir who also sang with correct accents in Church.[9]

The tribal religious belief system seemed to have been influenced. I would like to mention one example from the Santals. The Santal myth related that *Marang Buru* and others, the chief disciples of *Sing bonga* became discontented and they rebelled against his master the *Sing bonga* or Supreme being. The *Sing bonga* out of anger drove all of them from heaven to earth.[10] It appears that we are listening to a modified version of Biblical stories depicting the fall of the Angels.[11] Similarly about the creation of the Hos, the Mundas and the Santals we find that supreme God *Sing bonga* created a boy and a girl. They drank *illi* (Rice beer) which excited them with passion and thus the world was peopled.[12] In this also we find an echo of the Christian belief about the creation of nature and human being.[13]

Next major influence was in the field of education. The tribals of Chotanagpur did not have the tradition of imparting literate education. However, they learnt the lessons of how to lead their life through their *Gitiora, Dhumkaria, Akhara* (youth dormitories) only. This was both their mode of socialization and materialization. But with the spread of Christianity missionaries introduced modern literate culture in tribal life.[14] They founded many schools, technical and agricultural centres, colleges in the whole of Chotanagpur. These institutions were set up not only at Ranchi but at Chaibasa, Hazaribagh, Lohardaga, Murhu, Govindpur, Burju, Tapkara, Mandar, Simdega, Basia etc.[15] Not only that medical dispensaries, clinics and hospitals were also set up in Ranchi, Hazaribagh, Murhu, Itki, Gumla, Lohardaga, Huluhundu, Mandar by different Christian denominations.[16]

Christian missionaries and converts were pioneers in giving the tribal language a written and literary form. Many thousands of new hymns and songs were composed and sung in Christian worships, festive occasions and in all the important functions.[17] Furthermore, many missionaries published literature about the history, language and other aspects of the life of tribals. Father Lievens' Munda World, Father Hoffmann's Encyclopaedia Mundarica, Father J. Deeney's Ho Dictionary and Ho Grammar etc. are some of the texts which encouraged the indigenous people to develop distinct linguistic identities.

Combined effects of new religion and education shaped and moulded tribal life in many other ways. The Cathedral at Ranchi, other Churches and schools and hospitals added a new dimension to tribal religious life. The centre of life and activities now shifted from *Sarna,* the natural grove, to the Church. The mode of living of the converted tribals registered a change. It was first witnessed among those, who were employed by the Church and lived on Church campus. They were provided with pucca houses with windows and chimneys for letting out smoke. This change in living condition introduced a new vision and attitude to life and it provided a fresh strength to face the challenges of life around them.[18] Others were soon inspired. Those converts who lived in the villages their houses were much more neat and clean than those of the non-Christian tribals.[19]

This was followed by new items of use in tribal Christian houses. One could find a lot of fancy goods such as fountain pen, goggles, torches, cheap camera and radio. Cheap variety of soaps, slippers, plastic comb, powders became essential items used by Christian tribal ladies.[20] Regarding their dress converted Mundas living near town began to wear mill-made clothes. Some used to wear coat and maintained clocks also, as they became time conscious.[21] Similarly in the villages Christian ladies covered the whole body by using jumper or *jhula* while generally the non-converted tribal ladies left that portion exposed.[22] Generally the Mundas were in the habit of wearing long hair but after conversion they started keeping short hair.[23]

Besides general education the tribal students undertook technical trainings also. Some of the institutions imparting training in lace-making, embroidery also.[24] In Chaibasa, girls learnt the art of weaving.[25] This helped tribals to seek new vocations in life. With this an over dependence on agriculture decreased among them. Similarly after getting education the Church also provided employment to the converted tribal students. They became priests, teachers, nurses, cooks, chaprasis, malis and so on.[26] Not only in missionary institutions but they were employed in government institutions also as a teacher, munshis, surveyors, school inspectors etc.[27]

Moreover, both tribals and non-tribals learnt how to play hockey, football, basket ball etc. For example, the S.P.G. Mission hockey team of Ranchi, consisted of tribal students, was so strong that it once won the Hockey Challenge Cup at

Ranchi as well as in Calcutta also. In Ranchi in 1895 a Blind School was set up later on known as St. Michael Blind School where the blind men were trained in industrial work like cane, bamboo and mat making. Reading and writing were also taught after the Brail system.[28]

The Christian names were so popular among the tribals that even non-Christian tribal people of this region named their children after the Christian names like John, James, Nelson, Dhanmasih etc.

Christianity removed some social evils also. It was a belief among the tribes that if one became a Christian the witches and spirits would not disturb them. This lessened their faith in witchcraft. Moreover, Christianity also helped its adherents to combat alcoholism, which was very much prevalent in this region.[29]

Some of the socio-religious movements bore the imprint of Christianity. During Birsa movement we find that in Birsait religious prayer meetings were same as the ones Birsa himself attended during his mission school life at Chaibasa. Similarly his miraculous power for curing diseases, thursday prayer had their roots in Christianity.[30] The Kherwar movements in Santal Pargana (1872-79) were also to some extent influenced by Christianity. It is said that Bhagirath, the leader of the movement, was either himself a Christian or was educated in a Christian educational institution.[31] Because he preached his followers to observe certain perceptive which was much like the ten commandments.[32] Sunday prayers, healing from sick etc. bear clear influence of Christianity.[33]

Like their socio-cultural life political life of the tribals came under Christian influence. The tribals who took education at missionary schools and others became aware of the rights and privileges.[34] So when the zamindars, landlords and thikadars exploited the Munda Sardars of Ranchi and Bandgaon they revolted against these Dikkus. Thus the Sardari Larai started between 1858 and 1895. This movement received both moral and material support of local missions. Moreover, the leaders of Sardari movement were mostly Christian educated tribals.[35] Before that during the Revolt of 1857-58 the missionaries had helped tribal Christians when the zamindars and moneylenders had oppressed these people. Not only this whenever the zamindars usurped their land and oppressed them[36] the prevalent belief among the tribals was that by becoming Christians one could get rid of all these exploitations.[37]

Sardari Larai failed but soon a charismatic leader emerged, who was Birsa Munda. He was also a Christian. He received his early education at Burju Mission. Later on he was educated at Chaibasa Lutheran School from 1886 to 1890. His school life at Chaibasa and missionary education built his personality. Very soon he became a dominant force among his people.[38] He fought for establishing Abua Raj i.e. the Munda Raj. Though he and most of his followers were Christians yet he attacked even Christian Mundas and missionaries on Christmas eve of 1899 for their alleged support to the government and zamindars.[39] He was afterwards caught and jailed, where he died on 9 June 1900.[40] But he was the man who encouraged the people of Chotanagpur to fight foreign elements, both British and Indians.[41]

In spite of all these one thing is to be noted that though the Kherwar movement and the Birsa movement were influenced by Christianity and they observed some of the Christian percepts in their own religious beliefs yet later on their faith in Christianity was shaken and they moved back again to their original faith. In the case of Birsa we find that he embraced Christianity first but due to non-co-operation of the missionaries towards his movements he, having been frustrated by the missionaries, reverted to his original faith. And the result was the emergence of a new movement which came to be known as a separate and distinct Birsait religion.

The present Jharkhand movement had its seeds in the little organization which was shaped by its founder J. Bartholomew, a young Christian orphan of Chaibasa. Bartholomew (some say he was a tribal orphan), who among the leaders of the Jharkhand movement, was perhaps the first who thought of the pitiful condition of the people. This prompted him to form an organization on the lines of Dacca Students' Union at St. Colamba's College, Hazaribagh, where he was a student in 1910.[42] He was the pioneer of the present Jharkhand movement. Later on Chotanagpur Unnati Samaj, Chotanagpur Catholic Sabha, Chotanagpur Adivasi Mahasabha and lastly Jharkhand

Party emerged as the most powerful political organizations of Chotanagpur.[43] These movements were the concrete examples of the attempts to assert the right over land under the direct impact of the Christian mission and the Christian Church.[44]

In the beginning all the leaders of these movements like Theble Oraon, Rev. Joel Lakra, Paul Dayal, Bandi Oraon etc. were tribals. But after Jaipal Singh entered the scene, the Jharkhand movement became completely changed. Jaipal Singh was a Christian and educated at St. John College, Oxford.[45] On 9 March 1941 at Ranchi he for the first time openly demanded a separate state for the tribal people. Like Birsa he also very soon became popular among the tribals who regarded him as *Marang Gomke* (the Supreme Leader).[46] In the year 1950 he formed Jharkhand Party and became unchallenged leader of the tribals of Chotanagpur upto 1963 when his party merged in Congress Party.[47] Even after that Justin Richard, N.E. Horo, S.K. Bage and Theodore Bodra were some of the tribal Christians who became frontline leaders of Jharkhand movement.[48] They played an important role in achieving Jharkhand state.

Thus we see that Christianity has always been one of the major catalysts in ushering modernity in Chotanagpur. Even today role of Christian missions and tribal Christians in spreading education and political consciousness continues to be a significant force in the public life of Chotanagpur.

Notes and References

1. S.P. Sinha, *Conflict and Tension in Tribal Society,* New Delhi, 1993, p. 96.
2. K. Shital, *Chotanagpur Ki Kalisia Ka Britant,* Allahabad, 1940, pp. 4-9.
3. S.C. Roy, *The Mundas and their Country,* Calcutta, 1912, p. 228.
4. Sinha, *Conflict,* pp.106-107.
5. *Ibid.*, pp. 97-99, 103; Shital, *Chotanagpur,* pp.16-24.
6. N. Kumar, *Ranchi District Gazetteer,* Patna, 1970, p. 56; Sinha, *Conflict,* p.129.
7. Ramkumar Tiwari, *Jharkhand Ka Bhugol,* New Delhi, 2000, p. 241.

8. Nirmal Minz, Transforming Effects of Christianity on the Tribals of Chotanagpur, in P. Dash Sharma (ed), *The Passing Scene in Chotanagpur,* Ranchi, 1980, pp. 77-78.
9. E.T. Dalton, *Tribal History of Eastern India* (Original title Descriptive Ethnology of Bengal), Delhi, 1973, p. 257.
10. D.N. Majumdar, *A Tribe in Transition,* Calcutta, 1937, p.126.
11. *Ibid.,* p. 126; *The Bible,* W.M. Collins Sons and Co. Ltd., Great Britain, 1952, The Revelation, Chapter 12 : 7-9.
12. Majumdar, *A Tribe,* p.126.
13. The Bible, *Genesis,* Chapter 1-4.
14. Manoranjan S.K. Paty, *Christian Education in Tribal Chotanagpur,* Paper presented at the Conference on the "History and Philosophy of Christian Education in India", held on 26th to 30th May 2000 at Christu Jyoti College, Krishnarajapuram, Bangalore, pp. 3-5.
15. Kumar, *Ranchi District Gazetteer,* pp. 464, 540.
16. *Ibid.,* pp. 539-541.
17. Minz, Transforming Effects, p. 77.
18. *Ibid.,* p. 75.
19. Roy, *The Mundas,* p. 268.
20. L. P. Vidyarthi and Makhan Jha, *Growth and Development of Anthropology in Bihar,* New Delhi, 1979, p. 80.
21. Roy, *The Mundas,* pp. 365, 367.
22. Majumdar, *A Tribe,* p. 21.
23. Roy, *The Mundas,* p. 369.
24. *Ibid.,* p. 351.
25. Sinha, *Conflict,* p. 160.
26. Minz, Transforming Effects, p. 77.
27. Roy, *The Mundas,* p. 351; Fr. Emmanuel Barla, *Political Socialization of Mundas,* Satya Bharti Publication, Ranchi, p. 34.
28. Roy, *The Mundas,* pp. 263-265.
29. Dalton, *Tribal History,* p. 257; John McDougall, *Land or Religion,* New Delhi, 1985, pp. 200-201; Sinha, *Conflict,* p.101.
30. Stephen Fuchs, *Rebellious Prophets,* Bombay, 1908, p. 28.
31. Sinha, *Conflict,* p. 214; MacDougall, *The Land,* p. 90; Fuches, *Rebellious,* p. 53.
32. MacDougall, *The Land,* p. 72; The Bible, Exodus, Chapter 20.
33. Fuchs, *Rebellious,* p. 56.
34. Paty, Christian Education, p. 10.
35. Peter Tete, *A Missionary Social Worker in India,* Ranchi, 1986, pp. 13-17. MacDougall, *The Land,* p. 67.
36. *Ibid.,* pp.13-17.

37. Captain E.T. Dalton to the Secretary, Government of Bengal dated 25 March, 1859, No. 70, Paper related to Chotanagpur Agrarian Disputes.
38. Suresh Singh, *The Dust Storm and Hanging Mist,* Calcutta, 1966, pp. 32-38.
39. Fuchs, *Rebellious,* p. 32.
40. Singh, *The Dust Storm,* p. 130.
41. Fuches, *Rebellious,* p. 34.
42. L.P. Vidyarthi, *Cultural Contours of Tribal Bihar,* Calcutta, 1964, p. 153; Sinha, *Conflict,* p. 162.
43. *Ibid.,* pp. 155-159.
44. Minz, Transforming Effects, p. 79.
45. Sinha, *Conflict,* p. 286.
46. *Ibid.,* p. 284.
47. S. Bosu Mullick, 'The Jharkhand Movement, A Historical Analysis', in Mrinal Miri (Ed), *Continuity and Change in Tribal Society,* Shimla, 1993, pp. 458-459.
48. Sinha, *Conflict,* pp. 303-312.

11

How should we resolve Value-laden Practical Problems in Changing Tribal Societies?

Debashis Guha

Some social problems should be better called 'practical problems of great urgency', i.e. problems emerging and crystallizing in a society having tremendous pragmatic value, which even if we like it or not, we have to face because they are so real, so unavoidable, so down-to-earth that they affect us in some way or other. However, they affect those people more who are directly involved in tackling such problems in the day-to-day practical situations in the society. To be precise, they are 'professionals' of various fields. Hence, we have at hand many unavoidable practical problems of great urgency for the professionals in our societies. Needless to say that in a tribal society or tribal societies the professionals face many such practical problems, which are extremely challenging because tribal societies are marked by their uniqueness, distinctiveness and therefore, prop up distinctive practical problems, which a non-tribal society may be bereft of.

All practical problems are however not value-laden, most of them are in fact value-free, i.e. most of them pose a practical challenge to professionals insofar as to find out the mere nitty-gritty or how-to-do-such-and-such-things but not why such and such things *should* be done or *ought* to be done. Some practical problems are 'value-laden' because they raise primarily ethical questions of rightness, oughtness, desirability, goodness and so on. We ask, what is good or right in doing such and such things before we (professionals) go for the nitty-gritty? Interestingly, a skeptic may ask, do we really ask that? The answer should be an honest 'no' with a caution, that this was exactly expected from us (professionals) or that we should have cared for such questions. The reason is fairly simple; we should give precedence to ought questions or value-laden practical problems for it is a pre-requisite of professionals in a civilized society. It is not that caring about such things makes us civilized overnight but it is a strong basis of civilization. Clearly, a strong basis of civilization is to take care of desirability questions before professionals in a society take steps for doing certain things, which in the long run affect the whole public life. Once we press on with such simple inquiries like, but what is good or right or just in doing X? Every other professional who faces these problems comes out with explanations about the rightness, the goodness and the oughtness of doing X. As we know that there are many distinctive value-laden practical problems for the professionals of the tribal land as well, they should address the desirability questions. But how one has to do this is a trifling problem.

Another point is that considering moral trifles within a society demands moral resolution as well. Who loves to live in impasse? This is the reason that our professionals through moral resolutions of these problems should try to approach practical decision-making, a process that is itself moral. Hence decision-making becomes morally grounded when our professionals strive for moral resolution of value-laden practical problems. Here a skeptic may ask do we ever do that? No perhaps, but we 'ought' to do that. Skeptic's other bad question is, 'what great thing will an ethicist do by doing such things?' And what if he did not do such things?' Our reply is simple. If such things were not done by ethicists, someone else will do. But ethicists make a good party in moral resolution for they are better trained in doing some such things, which others cannot do as effectively. We will come to it later on. Moreover, considering moral impasse and resolving them is not a means towards creating a utopian moral society overnight by ethicists (as if ethicists have taken up that burden). Rather, ethicists *should* undertake this practical task as well for it is one of their moral bindings to consider such problems in a civilized society, however not in isolation but with all interested parties and involving other professionals.

With this we come to understand that in any tribal society, professionals *should* apply their *ethical knowledge* with regard to ethical impasse and frame some such decision-making rules that a value-laden practical problem finds a moral pathway to resolution. This is thus *applying ethics*, where professionals, who are non-philosophers, and philosophers as well come together in an interdisciplinary venture to resolve moral impasse. But the problem is how to do such things? This is the problem of *methodology* of ethical application. We shall come to it now.

Broadly speaking, there are two models of ethical application for value resolution and for framing value-oriented decision-making rules, viz. the *deductive* and the *inductive* models. However, I will try to justify that rather than accepting them we should go for 'inter-subjective corroboration'. The 'deductive model' is a body of a number of methodologies of ethical application, i.e. they form a family of models so to say. Among them, we have the *fruits-of-the-theory*, the *engineering*, the *teaching-across-the curriculum* and the *casuistic models* of ethical application whereas the 'inductive model' is relatively simple and does not consist of a family of models. The above models are called 'deductive' insofar as all of them agree to have based on a fixed set of ethical principle or principles which are well justified and are accepted to be the valid premises of *deriving* what *should* or *ought* to be done in a *particular practical value-laden situation*. The result is the formulation of decision-making rules, which are at best deduced truths from valid premises, and therefore, need to be followed without further disagreement. Next, almost all of them tend to agree that the whole process of deductions of decision-making rules for professionals begs ethics expertise. So without unilateral ethicists' effort, application of ethics and value-resolution does not happen. The method is thus deriving *fruits* or *consequences* out of any ethical theory or theories, which demands ethics experts or engineers, who from their tool-box (knowledge of ethical theories) pick proper tools (theories) at appropriate situations (value-laden practical cases) to resolve them to formulate dos and don'ts for professionals. This is *ethical engineering* by ethics experts. The model thus encourages *teaching of ethics across the curriculum* by experts to non-philosophers or professionals in order to enrich their ethical knowledge, thus enabling them to resolve ethical crises. Such experts are then like the *casuists* of the old Church era who would enjoy finding out pathways to moral crises by dint of their wise ethical guidance. Being guides, engineers, preachers, teachers and so on, ethics gurus are thus *sophists* who think they have a sacred task to teach how to become ethical. This is thus moral chauvinism and a wholly misconceived ideology that applying ethics aims at turning the whole population ethical. Alas! This does not happen and this should not happen in a civilized nation.

In ethical application, we must not forget that what ethics experts say about the dos and don'ts of, for instance, harnessing rivers in tribal areas for mega-power production will not be accepted by the tribal people, the engineers, the politicians, the environmentalists as if they are value-free foolheads. This is because ethical application is *not application of any one or many ethical theory or theories* like utilitarianism *by ethics experts* in an artificial manner so as to resolve value-laden problems like the one mentioned above. Many philosophers, who think that ethical application is just this, are skeptical about philosophers doing such things. Really the skeptics are correct in saying that when our house is on fire, we do not think about why water extinguishes fire. And when our house is on fire we do not wait for chemists to come to teach us. Hence, ethical application is just not ethicists' business, it needs other parties as well, should be the conclusion, and not that applying ethics is absurd as the skeptics think.

When we come to 'inductive model', we find that ethical chauvinism is still lurking in a different garb. Here the ethics experts put themselves in different value-laden practical situations and find out what should professionals do now or what act 'now' would save the situation without however referring to any moral theory because that is impractical. Nevertheless, such *contextualists* would further find out through an intriguing process of *generalization*, which theory or theories most likely should be established as *working hypothesis* in practical situations. Such working ethical hypothesis may be nonetheless of more academic value for in real life cases they hopefully fall out. Therefore deductions from principles are not needed. Contextual moral calculus by ethics experts is primary, which may further be generalized to frame ethical principles.

There are several problems with the contextualists. One is that ethics experts cannot and need not alone assume powers to find out the dos and don'ts in different practical situations. Next, even if they are able to do such things sometimes, and end up in framing general working ethical hypothesis, the hypothesis so framed will be at best probably true and need not be termed as absolutely justified *general* theory or theories at all. Moreover, what only an ethicist formulates as a working hypothesis will have little or no value to society at large in real cases of moral resolution unless the ethicist takes a full circle to fall in the line of teaching-preaching and say that they would teach all such theories to our poor professionals so that they are able to resolve ethical impasse. Hence, ethical application is not framing working ethical hypothesis for professionals by ethics experts and educating them about all that. Take this; what will an ethicist do when he is faced with a problem like, whether or not rivers in tribal land should be harnessed for mega power production? Can he really look for a number of situations with regard to this issue unless he goes for a thorough public debate? Certainly not. And this takes us to what should be done in ethical application.

In fact, we have to go for ethical corroboration or what I call *inter-subjective corroboration*. The basis of this methodology is that every sane, grown up social being in a civilized society possesses ethical knowledge through *ethical experience* because every individual lives in a teeming social interrelationship, which covers all biotic and abiotic life forms. We are thus living in an ecological community wherein through our voluntary actions, interactions and the voluntary actions of otherselves, we are constantly having ethical experience, i.e. *experience pertaining to what should be done*, what should not be done, what is right, wrong, good, bad, just, duty and obligation. Within the constant flux of social change, our divergent moral experiences contribute to diverse moral knowledge. Therefore, moral knowledge is knowledge pertaining to morality, i.e. pertaining to goodness, rightness, oughtness etc. and *not* merely knowledge of ethical theories like utilitarianism and so on. Only a few people called 'trained philosophers' may have such knowledge of ethical theories, which is however, no great advantage in moral resolution because I think, moral resolution does not happen without corroboration of ethical views. For this, one has to go for a number of moral dialogues, where disagreements may gradually give way to agreements. It is due to this that we have to distinguish between 'knowledge of theoretical ethics' and 'ethical knowledge'. Nevertheless, we must also keep in mind that the former is one field in which we have ethics experts but the latter is not restricted to experts, it is a virtue of sane, grown-up human beings. To this I must add that the established theories of theoretical ethics are neither a priori nor intuitive findings from the bolt of the blue. No expert mind can ever establish an ethical theory if there is no *empirical* anchor. Therefore, moral experience and moral knowledge in general is needed for the establishment of general ethical principles. For this however, like contextualists, we need not artificially follow a method of placing ourselves in various moral situations and then subsume a moral theory through induction. We are all there in the social life, acting, reacting, influencing and influenced, and thus come to realize the questions of desirability. Others, who are wise men of gifted powers of *abstraction,* go still further for theoretical constructions and justifications of what they call, 'theories of ethics'. Non-philosophers are perhaps different insofar as they do not or could not go for such theoretical constructs. Rather, they are bound to their practical ethical knowledge or what Aristotle called 'practical wisdom' or 'praktike' to resolve moral crises.

Interestingly, moral resolution of value-laden practical problems by moral dialogues ought to be initiated in our society by a party. Ethicists are important here. They are perhaps the *best trained parties* to *frame questionnaires* which are value-oriented, *arrange* a number of *moral dialogues* with concerned non-philosophers or professionals regarding a value-laden issue, *moderate the dialogue*, try to *show* if there is any *discrepancy in one's moral view* and let professionals come to a *moral consensus* or help in *inter-subjective corroboration.* This may further end up in *formulation* of *decision-making rules* of great pragmatic value. Such rules may fizzle out or change with the changing value-trends but every time we find a resolution through this method, it is firmly grounded on a method that is moral, it does not beg moral chauvinism of ethics gurus.

It is clear therefore, that we have for us one valuable method to resolve the issue of whether or not mega power production should be allowed in changing times in Jharkhand. I have tried to do exactly this during 1997 to 2000 when I considered not one but several such issues with a number of professionals in this area. Needless to say, one issue, which is really troubling us for a long time is the one mentioned above. In recent times it has gained centre stage once again as the government is again pressing with the Koel-Karo project. I have followed exactly the method I mentioned just now with professionals in the moral debates and most satisfying fact is that I have now in hand what people of this tribal land feel. (I will come out with the findings in the near future. I must say it may not please many of us, particularly those, who have been pleased at the fall of the Narmada Bachao Andolan). But that is a different story. As the paper is about justification of applying ethics along with a proper model of application, I should better focus my attention on why the problem in consideration, i.e. harnessing rivers in tribal regions etc. is value-laden and needs moral resolution through application of ethics following inter-subjective corroboration.

The problem is a practical one insofar as the government and those responsible for power generation and distribution in the tribal regions are trying their best to find out the ways or steps for enough power generation and distribution. Of course the bone of contention being harnessing the rivers flowing through tribal regions by erecting big dams and so on, the result of which are, forest depletion, elimination of a perennial river-valley civilization, cultural depletion and obvious pollution when the production-distribution is at full force. Nevertheless, the reasons of such practice may be many. One is very popular; it is 'multipurpose'. But its life may be 100 odd years at best, giving pleasures to a few having purchased power. But time has shown that such projects turned out to be "multiple failures" in a short time. Yet, the bigger is the project and the longer it goes, the greater is the cost and the greatest is the benefit to a few, those knowing to tap it. The higher is the dam elevation, the higher is someone's income. So we face a serious practical problem.

But the problem is value-laden as well insofar as it raises serious questions of 'desirability'. I wonder how a conscious civil person could fail to see that. It raises questions like, should we go for such large-scale river-valley projects for mega powerhouses in tribal areas, playing with the whole aquatic life of these regions? And we know that rivers in areas like Jharkhand are hilly, they are mostly rain-fed and do not have the expected flow throughout the year. Hence, the main tone is an ethical tone of why such steps should be taken before we have plunged into doing such things. For this, such 'power-talk' involves 'ethics talk' which needs proper ethical resolution.

Interesting is, who will resolve? The ethicists alone cannot do it. Not leaving the politicians of course, the policy makers, the whole group of people involved in power production and distribution and no doubt, common people of these regions, the tribal population, whose houses will be plundered first and the non-tribal people as well. Now if we involve all of them in moral resolutions it naturally points at moral dialogues, resolutions through corroboration of moral views and taking decisions. For this, the ethicists have a moral responsibility to come to arrange such debates. What is unphilosophical about it? If our philosopher friends want to be more philosophical take this.

Ethicists have another role to play, which is 'post-corroboration analysis', i.e. analyzing the moral intricacies of the dialogues, which reflects established or non-established ethical theory or theories and their practical value. We also come to know the practical value of such and such well-established or not so well-established moral theory and theories. If we teach these to our professionals, it may have a *purely theoretical value* no doubt but that is not an imperative for applying ethics. The greater teaching is needed for philosophers, particularly ethicists and, that is, ethics is all good to read and no good to apply is a great misconception. Similarly, to apply ethics is to apply ethical theories is another misconception. Beware of ethical chauvinism.

12

Value, Valuation and Tribal Society

Padmaja Sen

Introduction

Tribal life has so far been subjected to a probing by the social sciences, be it anthropology, history, sociology or economics. Though they make an in depth study of different aspects of tribal life surprisingly they have not yet undertaken the study of value oriented problems or for that matter the value-consciousness among tribals. Even if some of them have broached this[1] they have only made a cursory reference and that too not very consciously. It is safer to accept at the outset that it is not the main purpose of this paper to trace the history of the concept of value as such, neither do I intend to deliberate on various theoretical positions taken by philosophers on this issue. Rather I intend to focus on the value-consciousness of the tribal society of Jharkhand by identifying some value-laden problems which are otherwise understood as mere societal or political problems but which invariably refer to the value-consciousness latent in the psyche of tribal people. Hence the question what may be the possible reasons for this omission on the part of social scientists? I propose two plausible reasons. First is the general assumption that being concerned with facts per se as opposed to value, social sciences ought to be value-neutral. Secondly, it may be due to a grave misconception that the tribal society lacked value-consciousness in the sense generally understood. Let us consider these standpoints.

First let us examine the common assumption regarding value neutrality of social sciences. Are they really so value neutral as to be justified in interpreting a value-laden problem as a mere objective social or political problem? I would like to answer in the negative. It was Albrecht Ritschl, who started the debate between fact and value. He differentiated the sciences as factual and value oriented as they used judgment of fact or judgment of value. But he also recognized that this dichotomy is not tenable to a great extent. He observes 'value judgments therefore are what determine all connected knowledge of the world... Attention during scientific observation... always declares that such knowledge has a value for him who exercises it.'[2] Be it natural, biological or social, all scientific inquiries depend on the choice of the inquirer and value-orientation is inevitably inherent in the inquirer's selection of material for investigation itself. His choice is determined by culture-centric values. It is in this sense that Max Weber points out that social sciences are cultural sciences. They are the disciplines, which analyze the phenomena of life in terms of their cultural significance, and the concept of culture is a value concept. Empirical reality becomes 'culture' to us because and insofar as we relate it to value ideas.[3] Thus, neither the subject matter nor the method of social sciences is value-neutral. Perhaps an instance from a contemporary real life situation will substantiate my argument.

Recently a hot debate ensued around the transvaluation of the retention of Wilkinson's Civil rules in Kolhan. It brought the question, whether or not these rules should continue to govern Kolhan, in forefront. I shall make a little historical reference in order to make the value-ladenness of this problem more intelligible. These rules were first introduced for the whole of Chotanagpur except Kolhan. When Kolhan was brought under British control in 1837 the rules came into operation in Kolhan also. This set of civil rules was procedural ones, which prepared the framework of civil justice. The features were ready and expeditious justice, the induction of the tribal Manki-Munda system of governance and rule through tribal customs. These kept Kolhan beyond the jurisdiction of the Civil Procedure Code. This way the Hos of Kolhan have retained their particular identity so far administering civil justice is concerned.[4]

The retention of the Rules has created a problem, which may be viewed mainly as having a social and administrative relevance. But a deeper insight will show that the problem has in fact a deep value-ladenness, which prompted people to revaluate the rules in terms of its 'value for life' as suggested by Nietzsche. The concern regarding the extent to which the rules are conducive or detrimental to the preservation and enhancement of Kolhan, ultimately brings us face to face with a value-oriented question viz. does Wilkinson's Rules hold good for Kolhan people in ultimate assessment? Here we will take into account conflicting values represented by two types of people tribals and non-tribals living in Kolhan. Tribals rather the Hos think that these rules not only provide cheap and expeditious justice but more so the British administered them through their men and customs, which they prize most. Hence they should be retained.

Now not only the selection of Wilkinson's Rules as the subject matter of research by a social scientist but also the method adopted by him for this research is bound to be affected by the cultural relevance of tribal society of Kolhan. There is a great contemporary debate whether social sciences can at all be purely objective in approach. It is argued that any human mediation into social issues cannot avoid a subjective approach simply because a subject (social scientist) himself is the product of his culture which has an essential reference to value.

The Concept of Value in Tribal Society

The main objective of my paper, which I shall now seek to enumerate, is to focus on the value-consciousness of the tribal people of Jharkhand. The question is do they possess a value-consciousness or do they not? The answer to this question depends on how we understand value or value-consciousness. If we understand value in the Platonic sense of the term it can be said that tribal society lacked value-consciousness. Plato conceived the Idea of Good, the supreme value, as the culmination of the Ideal world. According to him values are extra-mental eternal realities which are totally unaffected by the empirical facts of the world or for that matter by the feeling, desire, passions or the needs of a person who intuits upon them.

Kant also holds a similar view when he declares autonomy of the Good Will and asks to perform duty for duty's sake. Plato, Kant, Sidgwick and Moore believed in a purely ontological concept of value. This view endorses a value-consciousness, which is assumed in a total isolation from real life situations. The tribal society of Jharkhand does not seem to uphold such a non-naturalist image of value. It seems quite natural that tribal society lacks such a complicated and intricate ontological concept of value. Hence from this point of view they may be said to be bereft of value-consciousness.

There may however be altogether a different angle of viewing this whole affair. If we take recourse to our experience we find that the awareness of value is as old as the human existence itself. We all can vouch of the presence of a judge sitting right within our hearts and determining the value of the objects as good or bad in relation to our feelings, passions, interests or needs, a judge who is constantly evaluating the intentional actions of people around us, pronouncing their actions to be right or wrong, good or bad according as they adhere to or are averse to the standard accepted in the society or culture of which we are a part. Viewed from this empirical point value seems to be deeply rooted in human choice, passions, drives and dispositions. As such value marks the whole behavioural pattern of an individual or society for that matter. The empirical aspect of value is rendered even more distinctly when R.B. Perry defines it as 'anything of interest to a human subject... It is that to which we are drawn to satisfy our needs, appetites, and drives.'[5] This approach makes it clear that values do not inhere in objects per se. An object has value for some one only if it is desirable for him. Hence the consciousness of value is sui generis. It consists in the practical attitude of some agent assumed towards an object or an intentional act in relation to his feelings, desires, interests, purposes and needs. It expresses his approbation or reprobation of an object or an intentional act in this relation. This empirical concept of value posits value right at the centre of concrete behavioural pattern of an individual or a society and tribal society is no exception to this. However, the value-consciousness of the tribal society can be better appreciated if we try to focus on the act of valuation adopted by the *adivasis*.

The Act of Valuation among the Tribes

Value is also used as verb to mean the act of evaluation in such expressions as 'to value', 'valuating,' 'valuation', or 'evaluation.' What is valuing or valuation? Obviously it is the act of determining the value of an object or an intentional act. It is an act of making a value-judgment. Now what precisely are we doing in passing a value-judgment upon an object or an intentional act especially from the empirical viewpoint dilated above? We are in fact judging an object or an intentional act in relation to human aspirations, needs or passions. When we relate this to tribal society and their valuation-process we are prompted to raise a two-fold question as to (1) how do the *adivasis* evaluate intentional human actions? and (2) what do they consider to be the highest value? While the first question relates the ethical or moral value, the second has a necessary reference to absolute value: the summum bonum of life.

First let us take up the ethical or moral value as envisaged by the *adivasis*. Although we do not find a formally formulated and developed code of conduct in tribal society in general, yet it can be said that their value-consciousness is deeply rooted in their tradition and socio-religious practices. It is however quite natural that the concept of morality in tribal society centres around its traditions and social customs. We can infer from the data provided by anthropologists, historians and sociologists that the Mundas, Oraons, Santals and Hos believe in some form of divine law working through the tribal social customs as the standard of morality. It is generally held that the knowledge of social customs and beliefs came down from their ancestors to whom it was supposed to have been bestowed by the Supreme God (*Singbonga, Dharmes* or *Haram*) Himself. The customs therefore manifest the divine's will and are accepted as the standard of moral conduct. Hence adherence to socio-religious customs is considered to be right and its violation as wrong. The socio-religious customs invariably aim at perpetuation of the family, clan and tribe. So any individual conduct, which is beneficent to the community, is considered good. The approach is obviously homogeneous and egalitarian. Equality, solidarity and peaceful co-existence not only within the tribe but also with the nature at large of which tribe is an essential part are highly valued moral ideals.

Let us take a judgment 'Every Ho should be treated as equal'. This is clearly a value-judgment which not only determines that the act of treating Hos as equals is good but it also means that the Ho society considers equality and homogeneity to be a cherished value. It has been accepted as a socio-cultural norm. This again has a reference to real life situation. We can find here the 'survival value' being the determining logic behind it. It reflects their concern for preserving their distinct socio-cultural identity, which they fear, may be threatened if their original egalitarian and homogeneous social order is disrupted.

It follows then that anything that is perceived as a possible threat to the community is considered to be wrong or evil and hence it invites the reprobation of the society. In this context I would invoke the contemporary debate around woman empowerment in Ho society.[6] The general perception in Ho society is that 'Women should not be given property right other than the usufructuary right allowed to them under customary law'. This is again a value judgment expressing the reprobation of Ho society towards women inheriting full property right, in view of their solidarity value. This value[7] implies that if tribal women are accorded post marital property right the essential intra village *killi* balance in the distribution of property will be disturbed adversely affecting solidarity and rhythm of Ho village life. Similarly given the property right, if a tribal woman marries a non-tribal man the tribal property will pass to a non-tribal or *Diku*. This will threaten the economic interest of Ho community and create existential crisis. Hence the modern value of equal property rights to male and female accorded by the Indian Constitution stumbles before the solidarity value of Ho society.[8]

The second question as to what do the *adivasis* consider to be the highest value inevitably leads us to some sort of formulation of absolute value. Though again in a society where formal philosophizing has not yet taken place it is difficult to come at an immediate conceptualization, yet it can be suggested on the strength of available body of literature that the Christian ideal of personal salvation or the Hindu ideal of *moksha* as the highest value are not original of the tribal society. In a sharp contrast to Advaita Vedantic or Buddhist approach the *adivasis* hold a very positive attitude towards this world of object and mundane life. The Supreme God has created this world and its objects, the life, the nature and the tribe. He is the source of all life and goodness. There is no other world known to exist other than this, no heaven or hell, neither a life beyond this.[9] Hence highest value is attached to things at two levels. From their prayers and socio-religious practices it is evident that at the level of physical world, abundant harvest, numerous cattle, healthy progeny and the general well being of the tribe are the most cherished values.

But at the same time there is another level – the level beyond this life, at which the most cherished wish of an *adivasi* lies in remaining in perfect harmony and peace with the tribe, nature at large and the supernatural powers. This wish is fulfilled when after death, through the rite of *umbul ader* the dead is reinstated and finally integrated in the family and the community to remain in the family *ading* with the ancestors forever. Evidently salvation or *moksha* through personal union with the Supreme is never sought as the highest value among the tribe. An individual is related to the Supreme only through the tribe or community as a part of cosmic nature. Hence the highest value is to be integrated with the nature in perfect harmony and peace.

Value and Changing Tribal Life

We are now in a position to relate the concept of value to changing tribal life. The ontological concept of value as absolute eternal entity does not admit of any change. Value as conceived by Plato transcends the empirical world, mundane life and its day-to-day affairs while value as empirically conceived is always at work in our real life situations. Naturally it admits a change in relation to human aspirations as and when the demand arises for such a change. The tribal society shows such changes in their valuation process due to their long association with Hinduism and Christianity, modern education and other socio-political factors. Equality and solidarity, strict adherence to customs, once cherished values, are not found in practice among modern educated *adivasis* as a rule today. The lack of the sense of individuality is also losing ground to accommodate a growing modern and articulate individual personality among them. The change is evident.

This will become clear when we diachronically evaluate the position of Ho women in society. During pre-colonial days it is understood that there was neither a demand nor allotment of maintenance plots to unmarried ladies. But the British theory of justice sought to introduce the notion of allotment of *khorposh* land to Ho women. It stuck not only to British notion of justice but had to concede to the tension brewing among Ho women who filed several court cases to claim right to property. The society also became supportive to this change in custom thereby creating a new empirical norm (value) of according maintenance plot to unmarried ladies. I do not see any contradiction in foreseeing a future when Ho society may fully enfranchise their women. The recent incidence of ladies becoming Mundas of villages is a step towards the emergence of a new value among the Hos.

This change in valuation is quite natural, even so when the social norms are accepted as the basis of moral evaluation. Besides the lack of a uniform moral standard they are subject to change with passing time. Some customs may even stand in contradiction to modern values and one may be proactive to correct them. Absolute values are only formal claims as in Kantian philosophy. In fact, every value-claim can very well be the subject of revision and correction. We can always question the validity of values recognized as social norms. Hence the problem of value also occurs in the sphere of values. The dichotomy between 'ought' and ' is', value and fact arises once again when we seek to determine the value of values, when the accepted values are taken as facts for the purpose of determining their value.

Notes and References

1. D. N. Majumdar, *A Tribe in Transition,* Longmans, Green and Co. Ltd., Calcutta, 1937; S. C. Roy, *Oraon Religion and Customs,*

Calcutta, 1972; A. Van Exem SJ, *The Religious System of the Munda Tribe,* Ranchi, 1982.

2. J. Hastings (ed), *Encyclopaedia of Religion and Ethics,* Vol. XII, T.T. Clark, New York, 1974, p. 585.

3. Max Weber, 'Objectivity in Social Sciences' in May Brodbeck (ed.), *Readings in the Philosophy of Social Sciences,* Macmillan, New York, 1968, p.88.

4. A.K. Sen (ed.), *Wilkinson's Rules : Context, Content and Ramifications,* Tata College Chaibasa, 1999.

5. Chhanda Gupta, 'Value and Social Science' in K. Roy and C. Gupta (ed), *Essays in Social and Political Philosophy,* ICPR, New Delhi, pp.75-93.

6. Ho society extends their women a limited right to enjoy property till their marriage or death. After marriage or death their properties revert back to near male relatives. See Dr. P. Sen, 'Roots of Gender Empowerment and Deprivation in Ho Society' in Dr. S. Mahanty (ed.), *Equity and Sustainability in Development of Tribal Areas,* Mahila College Chaibasa, 2000, pp. 17-24.

7. The following information owes to a discussion with Dr. A.K.Sen and reading of his unpublished monograph 'From Village, Elder to the British Judge: Custom, Customary Law and Ho Society.

8. For a detailed list of individual code of conduct regarded with disapproval and which invokes the displeasure of the community see Majumdar, A Tribe ; B. Tirkey, 'Oraon Ethical Values', Sevartham, Vol. 9, 1984, St. Albert's College, Ranchi, pp. 57-68.

9. Dr. P. Sen and Dr. A. K. Sen, 'Religion as Identity: Evolution of Religious Ideas among the Adivasis of Jharkhand', Special Issue on Philosophical Traditions in Regional Languages of India, Journal of Indian Council of Philosophical Research, New Delhi, pp. 243-254 (forthcoming).

13

Development
Conflicting Ideologies

S.N.M. Topno

It is very essential to focus our attention on some of the burning problems of the tribal people of Chotanagpur in the state of Jharkhand. These problems are related with land, water and forest.

The Chotanagpur plateau is one of richest areas in the whole country, rich in minerals with huge reserves of coal, iron ore, mica, bauxite, china clay and copper. It has a considerable reserve of manganese, limestone, atomic minerals etc. This region produces 48 per cent of bauxite, 45 per cent of mica, 100 per cent of kynite and 90 per cent of apatite. It is rich in forest resources also. Chotanagpur has 79 per cent of undivided Bihar's forest area, with Singhbhum having Asia's richest sal forests.

Ironically the natural wealth of the area contrasts palpably with the depressing poverty of the people who inhabit it. The tribals constitute a predominant part of the total population of Chotanagpur. But throughout the year the majority of them live in a state of starvation. On the other hand, non-tribal outsiders control the levers of power and economy, resulting in the relegation of the indigenes to a non-dominant position in their own land.

This region has been for ages the homeland of aboriginal peoples like the Santal, Munda, Oraon, Ho, Gond, Kharia, Bhuiyan, Bhumij, Birhor and others. These indigenous people of the area are also known as *adivasis,* which mean original settlers. Their identity and culture is rooted in their land, and around the natural setting they live in. It is this relationship, which constitutes the unique feature of *adivasi* culture. Their societies are community-based. Land is owned commonly. Community life is co-operative and is based on reciprocity. Any decision is taken jointly through consensus. Their society is considered to be classless and egalitarian. On the other hand, the societies around them are often highly exploitative, stratified, centralized, individualistic and anti-nature.

Tribals consider land as the mother of people. Therefore land cannot be owned, bought or sold. The resources are for all to use, though at sustainable regeneration level. But more than a bounteous material-provider, the land is also sacred. It is because the *adivasis* firmly believe that their ancestors still tread on this land. This intimacy with land has resulted in a vast repository of knowledge of the flora and fauna. As a part of their virtual communion with nature their food habits ensured their health. This knowledge is now appreciated by world outside and packaged into commercial products such as 'health foods', herbal medicines and 'holistic health' care.

The land formed the core of the education of the *adivasis* also. How to exist in harmony with nature is an ongoing learning process, which continues right through life. No other community can understand this essential link between the tribals and nature. They celebrate many festivals, which are based on nature. They consider earth as their mother, the trees the abode of their ancestors and river and mountains as their brothers. The tribal attitude to the conservation of forest and other natural resources follow community character because all the natural resources are meant for their livelihood and not merely as raw material.

Tribals, who constituted the first settlers in the Indian forests, still largely occupy forest regions where they have lived for long in relative isolation from the mainstream societies. They have an intimate relationship with the forest around them. Traditionally they have been dependent on the forest for food, fuel, housing materials and medicine. Every dwelling tribal group has a set of trees and plants often considered sacred, the commonest being the mahua and sal trees. These species have great economic value and are essential for their survival. In short we can say that the forest is a way of life for them.

Like land and forest natural sources of water are very dear to them. When they founded their villages they always kept in mind the proximity of the source of water. Rivers and springs had always been the great sustainer of *adivasi* civilization. As a predominantly agrarian people they used water to irrigate their lands for higher yield. This use of water coupled with the fish as a delicacy and for a few as a marketable item encouraged them even during colonial times to excavate ponds and bandhs.

Adivasi sensitivity around nature faced a serious challenge from a so-called modern and counter ideology of development that was based mostly on indiscriminate exploitation of nature for the supposed good of the humankind. Unfortunately that humankind does not include the indigenes. The result is their large-scale land alienation and displacement. The process, which began during British rule, continued unabated in independent India.

Like most other newly independent countries, India took for granted that the growth of the GNP was the real criterion of national development. Development, displacement and rehabilitation are inter-related. While the technical aspects are worked out, the problem of displacement and rehabilitation also arises. The number of those who have been displaced but not rehabilitated is over 11.5 million. While one discusses the dams that have displaced people without adequate rehabilitation, one must concentrate on the tribal belt, which is well known for its mineral wealth and forest. A very large number of displaced people unfortunately belong to the scheduled castes and tribes. It is desired that the problem of displacement of these marginal groups should be approached more humanely than giving them mere cash compensation.

The land acquisition is an example of state anarchy. It is not in accordance with the spirit of our Constitution. Acquisition of land becomes a certainty the moment a decision is taken about the establishment of the project. It is well known that 90 per cent of the coalmines are in tribal areas. But the tribals have no share in it. Neither do they have a share from the fruits of their land, nor the land itself. About 60 per cent of those dispelled by big dams are *Adivasis* and *Dalits.* Thus they have been deprived of their rightful possessions, often the only source of their living, in the name of national interest and progress.

The Land Acquisition Act does not contain any provision for rehabilitation. Natural justice demands that land acquisition and rehabilitation should serve public purpose and public welfare. One should not forget that the benefits of the big project financed by the World Bank would go basically to the big industrial houses and metropolises and not to those people who have been deprived. That is why the people of this area oppose the construction of such projects.

I shall cite the example of the Subarnrekha project, which caused large displacement of *adivasis* and others. It was conceived in 1974 at an estimated cost of Rs. 1.29 billion. The Ministry of Environment had not given clearance to the project and yet the Chandil dam has nearly reached completion. Apart from the question of environment the project has a shameful record of resettlement and habilitation, which continues to be an unsettled matter. In Icha dam of West Singhbhum affected persons protesting under the leadership of Gangaram Kalundia, a retired soldier decorated for bravery during the Indo-China war, have had a very bad experience. Lastly on 4 April 1992 he was brutally assaulted and murdered. In the present situation the protests are growing stronger and development projects face a crisis. The Koel-Karo project is the glaring example.

Land acquisition policy is generally discriminatory. It does not mean that natural resources are available only in areas where the *adivasis* live. This is also the area where the powerless live. The best coking coal of Jharia coal belt is under Jharia town, a small business township. But it has not yet been mined. On the other hand in the name of natural parks and sanctuaries the *adivasi* lands have been systematically taken away from them.

Not development alone, land alienation occurs due to other reasons. In order to integrate *adivasis* into the mainstream, the government has announced liberal privileges for non-tribals marrying *adivasi* women. This provision is used by the non-*adivasis* to buy *adivasi* land. The resultant land alienation is obvious. Moreover, the encroachment into *adivasi* sacred groves and graveyards has also been taking place since long. This totally distorts their cosmology and is a devastation of serious magnitude.

Before British rule *adivasis* enjoyed unhindered rights over the forest and its produce. But since colonial days *adivasi* existence, identity and culture have been subjected to the vested interests and brute force of state. The origin of conflict between the state and the tribals can however be traced to the colonial times. The setting up of reserved forest was the tool for exploitation of natural wealth of India to meet the demands of Britain. With the reservation idea we find denudation of forest for industrial, mining and other purposes. All these caused progressive diminution of the customary rights of the forest dwellers. Forest produce, which formed the life support system of tribals, are transferred to another group of people for whom they are only one of the inputs in the assembly line. Since British rule the tribals in Jharkhand have been denied of their right to forests. Dispossessed of their ancestral homelands, they had often been forced to quit their traditional villages. Exploitation and harassment by forest officials and zamindars had been another cause of tribal migration. At times tribals were even forced to carry forest officials on their shoulders when the latter went on tour of the forest areas. Tribal women were considered by forest officials and zamindars as objects to satiate their lust. Fearing exploitation and harassment *adivasis* had to leave their original homelands and to retreat to interiors. Unfortunately this story of dispossession and denial is repeated in independent India also.

The standard of living of the *adivasis* inevitably face decline as traditional sources of firewood and forest produce became increasingly scarce. Tribals became poorer and poorer. Deforestation has increased tribal indebtedness forcing them to sell much of what they collect often at a throw away price to the local merchants. In short today they have less access to the food they need from the forest and they do not earn enough to buy their food. Deforestation has again resulted in the destabilization of *adivasi* culture and economy. Its impact is felt more by the *adivasi* women than men because women play a more important role in tribal economy. Due to deforestation tribal women have to walk longer distances in search of minor forest produce and firewood. As forest produce become rarer tribal women have to seek alternate source of income to supplement the family diet often forcing them to migrate in search of livelihood. Due to deforestation the medicinal plants and herbs have been fast disappearing, which ultimately results in the deterioration of the physical health of the tribals in general, and women in particular. Tribals depend much on herbal medicines. The non-availability of the indigenous herbs has created a climate in favour of modern medicine, which continues to remain inaccessible to them.

For the *adivasi* to be displaced from the land of his ancestors has been an extremely traumatic experience because with this land goes his only means of livelihood, even his very culture. This is an invisible part of his identity. In Singhbhum district of Jharkhand at present one can see tremendous turmoil among *adivasis*. The turmoil is found not only in the economic and political fields but also socio-cultural spheres as well. This is manifested in various forms of such *Andolans* or people's struggles as: against the planting of teak and commercialization of forest; the *Dhan Kato Andolan* or forcible harvesting of paddy to get back the right on land illegally taken away from them; against the constructions of big dams and forcible evictions and against large scale alienation due to mining.

The above discussion shows the position of tribals and their relation with land, water and forest. In brief it can be said that the above existentialist problems in *adivasi* community need immediate solution. Conscious *adivasis* today question why they should loose their hearth and home in the name of national development? Why displacement and a living in the slums in the outskirts of big cities of the country, in abject poverty, illiteracy and poor health should be their fate in an independent country? I strongly feel that this is due to the lack of a more humane national tribal policy, a policy that should earnestly seek the welfare of the benighted millions. I would like to remind the policy makers of *Adivasi Panchasheel* (see the next essay for details) mooted by our first Prime Minister Pt. Jawahar Lal Nehru in 1957. These five principles admirably reflect noble intentions and good sentiments and are comparable to the best documents of this genre found elsewhere. Along with this, the

ILO-Convention 107 and 169, the Bhuria Committee Report and Panchayat Extension to the Scheduled Area Act, I believe, can be the milestone to develop tribal society.

References

Bosu Mullick, S., Edwin Jaydas, AntoAkkara and Anita Jaydas, *Indigenous Identity – Crisis and Reawakening,* Indian Confederation of Indigenous and Tribal Peoples, Navadin Prakashan Kendra, New Delhi, 1993.

Fernandes, Walter and Ganguli Thukral, Enakshi (ed), *Development, Displacement and Rehabilitation,* Indian Social Institute, New Delhi, 1987.

Indigenous and Tribal Solidarity, Indian Confederation of Indigenous and Tribal Peoples, 3rd General Assembly Meeting, 1997.

14

Approaches to Tribal Development
A Sociological Analysis
With a Special Reference to Jharkhand

Sunil Kumar Singh

On the map of India, the state of Jharkhand is recognized as a mineral rich and forest covered region. The culture of the tribals of Jharkhand is finely tuned to nature and is known for reciprocity, social equality, economic co-operation, consensus-based democracy, religious tolerance and collective presentation of art and music. This speciality of Jharkhand must be acknowledged and encouraged. Jharkhand earned statehood on 15 November 2000, as the 28th state of the Indian Union. Its territorial expanse is about 79,714 square kilometers. It has a population of 218.44 lakhs distributed in 22 districts. Among the states with a tribal population, Jharkhand stands third, the first and the second being Chattisgarh and Orissa respectively.

Right after the independence of the country efforts have been undertaken for the development and welfare of the tribal people. However, in comparison to the huge expenditure made and the scale of the measures adopted, success has not been up to our expectations. It is merely because the persons responsible for formulating the development plan have acted in a purely mechanical manner. Perhaps they do not consider the human and the social aspects. So the team, who prepare the development plan, must include sociologists and implement their suggestions. Only a sociologist is expected to have a deep insight into various aspects of development like social, cultural etc. We ought to properly understand the life and culture of the tribal people in order to conceive and implement the development programme in a better way.

The policies regarding the development of the tribal people must keep in view the following five basic principles suggested by Late Pt. Nehru. These principles are as follows:

1. People should develop along the lines of their own genius and we should avoid imposing anything on them. We should try to encourage in every way their own traditional arts and culture.
2. Tribal rights in land and forests should be respected.
3. We should try to train and build up a team of their own people to do the work of administration and development. Some technical personnel from outside the region will, no doubt, be needed especially in the beginning. But we should avoid introducing too many of them into tribal territory.
4. We should not over-administer these areas or overwhelm them with a multiplicity of schemes. We should rather work through their culture and not in rivalry with their own social and cultural institutions.
5. We should judge results not by statistics or the amount of money spent, but by the quality of human character that is evolved.

Considering the backwardness of the tribal people, the Articles 46, 275 and 339 of the Indian Constitution have made provisions to ensure their development and welfare. But the improvement in their status is not up to our expectations. The reason for this is that proper attention has not so far been given to the great diversity in the social status, historical background, cultural life and economic development among the different tribal groups inhabiting different geographical areas of India. Obviously, their problems are of different nature. Therefore, any measure adopted to overcome their problem must be region-specific and tribe-specific. Only then an overall multi-dimensional development of tribal people can be achieved in the present changing scenario. In this way we can prove right Pt. Nehru's words that planning, direction, consolidation and co-ordination are necessary but equally important is the need to create such circumstances where natural development is made possible at the lower level.

Often it has been complained that the tribals themselves oppose development plans which are aimed at their welfare. We must go to the roots of this opposition to find out a solution. I strongly feel that the local people should be fully informed about the development plan right from its inception i.e. in the beginning when the action plan is being formulated. Their suggestions should be invited and incorporated when the project report is finalized. The advantage of this participatory work is that the beneficiaries would take it as their own programme and not as something imposed upon them from outside. This will also create a harmony among the different sections of the society in that region, which is essential for any healthy growth. Since in most cases, the above mentioned facts or suggestions are not taken into account, mass opposition is faced at the time of the implementation of the action plan. As a result, the plan is either never implemented or implemented after many years have elapsed and many casualties have occurred. The much talked about Koel-Karo Hydel project is a burning example of such unimplemented projects.

Another suggestion is that it should be made mandatory for the non-tribal officers deputed in the tribal regions to acquire the knowledge of local/tribal languages. To ensure this the knowledge of any one local language should be made compulsory in the competitive examinations of Jharkhand state, as has been done in West Bengal, Orissa and the North-eastern states. This will help the officers to know the problems of the tribal region and to elicit the co-operation of the local people.

Tribals are deeply attached to their land. Agriculture has been their only means of subsistence for ages. But due to poverty and social obligations they are forced to transfer their land to others through legal as well as illegal ways. There are three basic reasons behind the illegal land transfer: (1) shortcomings in the judicial process (2) indigence of tribal people and (3) lack of awareness. To prevent the above evil it is necessary to review all the laws regarding holding of tribal land, remove complex procedures and ensure that the laws really serve the benighted.

To ameliorate the condition of tribals education can be of great help. However, the tribal education policy should be such as to remove their superstitions and prejudices so that they become receptive to the modernization process, without however snapping a link with their healthy traditions. But no less important is that they should be made aware of their constitutional rights and the means to protect them from exploitation.

Due to inadequacy of opportunities tribals are forced to migrate to other states viz. Punjab, Haryana, U.P., Delhi, Assam etc. for their livelihood. They are exploited socially economically and physically at their places of work. Better economic conditions in their own homelands would automatically relieve them of the problems associated with migration and the migration itself. For this all possible means should be explored for the employment of the tribals in the government as well as non-governmental spheres, cottage industries, handicrafts, forest-based industries etc. In this regard, the NGOs can play an important role.

Those who formulate the policies and implement them should never overlook the fact that tribals should be allowed to grow in tune with their 'own genius' and to preserve the sanctity of their culture.

Lastly, owing to its social, economic and cultural qualities Jharkhand can give direction to whole of India. We must consider the fact that "tribalness" is the extract of all serene human values. It should be nurtured at the national level. The concensual and participatory democracy in the tribal society is perhaps more democratic than the representational democracy in vogue. Despite several attacks on the tribal culture, "tribalness" has survived, which is the testimony to the liveliness of the tribal democratic society. Mahatma Buddha had preached about social liberation, a thing which is alive in the tribal consciousness. Such a situation, where all live together harmoniously and where nobody is unhappy is the basic concept of the tribal philosophy.

References

Ahmad, Ziyauddin, *Bihar Ke Adivasi,* Motilal Banarsidass, Delhi, 1988.

Dr. Ramdayal Munda ke sath Reporter Faisal Anurag Ki Vishesh Batchit, *Prabhat Khabar,* Ranchi.

Dutt, Balvir, 'Swarnarekha Project: Jamin Dibo Na, Taka Libo Na, Bandh Bandhte Dibo Na', *Prabhat Khabar,* Ranchi, dated December 10, 2001.

Hasnan, Nadin, *Janjatiya Bharat,* Jawahar Publishers and Distributors, New Delhi, 1997, pp. 153-196.

Kapur, Mastram, 'Janandolan Ka Rajniti Mein Hastakschep', Prabhat Khabar, Ranchi, dated 29 November, 2001.

Menon, P.S.K., 'Janjatiya Vikas, Nitiyan, Yojnaei Aur Karyakram', Yojna, New Delhi, Year 44, No.3, June, 2000, pp. 29-34.

Sahay, B.N., 'Janjatiya Kalyan', *Yojna,* New Delhi, Year 50, No. 10, January, 1997, pp.113-117.

Verma, U.K., *Bihar Ka Janjatiya Jivan,* Kishore Vidya Niketan, Varanasi, 1991.

Index